GRAMMAR FOR WRITING 3

AN EDITING GUIDE TO WRITING

Joyce S. Cain

ALWAYS LEARNING

PEARSON

Grammar for Writing 3: An Editing Guide to Writing

Copyright © 2012 by Pearson Education, Inc. All rights reserved.

No part of this publication may be reproduced, stored in a retrieval system, or transmitted in any form or by any means, electronic, mechanical, photocopying, recording, or otherwise, without the prior permission of the publisher.

Pearson ELT, 10 Bank Street, White Plains, NY 10606

Staff credits: The people who made up the **Grammar for Writing 3** team, representing editorial, production, design, and manufacturing are: Pietro Alongi, Rhea Banker, Christine Edmonds, Nancy Flaggman, Jaime Lieber, Amy McCormick, Massimo Rubini, Paula Van Ells, and Marian Wassner.

Cover design: Barbara Perez
Text design: Barbara Perez
Text composition: ElectraGraphics, Inc.
Text font: ITC Stone Serif
Cover photo credit: John Elk/Getty Images

Library of Congress Cataloging-in-Publication Data
Cain, Joyce S.
  [Eye on editing]
  Grammar for writing 1 : an editing guide to writing / Joyce S. Cain.
— 2nd ed.
      p. cm.
  Previously pub.: Eye on editing, 2001.
  Includes bibliographical references.
  ISBN 0-13-208898-3 — ISBN 0-13-208899-1 — ISBN 0-13-208900-9 1.
English language—Textbooks for foreign speakers. 2. English language—
Grammar—Problems, exercises, etc. 3. English language—Rhetoric—
Problems, exercises, etc. 4. Report writing—Problems, exercises, etc.
5. Editing—Problems, exercises, etc. I. Title. II. Title: Grammar
for writing one.
  PE1128.C25 2012
  808'.02—dc22

                                                    2011008774

ISBN-10: 0-13-208900-9
ISBN-13: 978-0-13-208900-5

PEARSON LONGMAN ON THE **WEB**

Pearsonlongman.com offers online resources for teachers and students. Access our Companion Websites, our online catalog, and our local offices around the world.

Visit us at **pearsonlongman.com**.

Printed in the United States of America

4 5 6 7 8 9 10–V092–16 15 14

Contents

To the Teacher

Grammar for Writing 3: An Editing Guide to Writing assists students in becoming accurate and fluent writers by focusing on the grammatical structures with which they most frequently have difficulty. It meets the needs of ESL and developmental writers who have acquired an advanced level of fluency yet still require guidance in detecting and correcting grammatical errors in their own writing. *Grammar for Writing 3: An Editing Guide to Writing* provides this guidance through exercises that focus on advanced grammatical structures, relevant writing topics, and academic vocabulary. Using this course, students will learn to apply appropriate grammar throughout the writing process, with emphasis on the final editing stage.

The concise grammatical explanations in *Grammar for Writing 3: An Editing Guide to Writing* are based on the most frequently occurring grammar errors of ESL and developmental students. The variety of editing exercises will help students begin to master the process of writing accurately and gain the confidence to edit their own written work. *Grammar for Writing 3: An Editing Guide to Writing* can stand on its own or serve as a supplement to reading, writing, and grammar classes. It is also a useful reference guide for students.

The primary goal of *Grammar for Writing 3: An Editing Guide to Writing* is to guide students as they navigate the writing and editing process on their own, enabling them to detect errors, analyze those errors, and use the correct forms in future writing. Students will develop the tools they need for the production of accurate, meaningful, and appropriate language by completing exercises based on academic topics, with vocabulary and sentence structures similar to those they are required to use in written compositions for their college courses. To this end, the grammar explanations and rules focus on those errors that are most prevalent in the writing of students at the advanced level.

Grammar for Writing 3: An Editing Guide to Writing is not intended to be a comprehensive grammar book. The grammar topics are based on an analysis of student writing errors and concepts necessary in academic discourse. Because it focuses on only specific problem areas, a cross-reference to two grammar books, *Understanding and Using English Grammar, Fourth Edition,* and *Focus on Grammar 5, Fourth Edition,* has been provided to assist those who would like further grammatical explanations.

Format and Content

Grammar for Writing 3: An Editing Guide to Writing has eleven chapters. Ten chapters focus on areas of grammar that are particularly problematic for advanced ESL and developmental writing students, while the final chapter provides further practice in all of these topics. The first ten chapters may be used in any order, and the final chapter may be drawn on as needed. It is possible to devote one week of class time to each chapter; however, depending on students' accuracy with each concept, there is enough material in the book when it is used as a supplemental text in a reading or writing class to fill a semester-long course.

Each of the first ten chapters is composed of four sections.

Building awareness. Students develop an awareness of the grammar concept by reading a brief description, observing how the grammar point is used in a brief piece of writing, and testing their prior knowledge with sentence-level items.

Grammar explanations. Charts and examples are used extensively to illustrate and visually reinforce the grammar points that are most important for student writers. When explanations are broken into subtopics, each subtopic ends with a short, sentence-level Self Check, which enables students to verify their understanding of the subtopic before moving on.

Editing practice. The next section is composed of exercises that focus on the task of editing written discourse—a skill students need to apply in their own writing. The exercises move students from the sentence to the discourse level, and from more guided to less guided tasks. Exercise 1, like the Pretest, asks students to locate errors in sentence-level items. Exercises 2–4 provide paragraph-level editing practice based on adapted academic student writing. In Exercise 2, errors are pointed out for students to correct; Exercise 3 generally requires students to supply the correct form of a given word; Exercise 4 asks students to locate and correct grammar errors in an unmarked piece of writing. Students are always told how many errors they must identify; however, just as in their own writing, they must scrutinize all sentences in order to edit the piece successfully. The exercises are appropriate for homework, in-class practice, or quizzes.

Writing topics. Each chapter ends with a writing task, designed for paragraph- to essay-length writing practice that asks students to use an outside source to support their ideas. Before students begin to write, they can read a sample. The sample not only models one of the writing topics suggested in the activity, but also provides students with an example of how to include an outside source to support the information presented in their writing. Once students have studied the content, organization, and language of the sample, they can easily move to their own writing, where they will also focus on the grammatical structures presented in the chapter. The writing topics are based on academic themes that are accessible to students without instruction on the content.

Chapter 11 consists of paragraph-level editing exercises that are similar to Exercise 4 in the earlier chapters. However, these paragraphs require students to edit for more than one type of grammar error at a time, providing them with further realistic practice.

The first appendix, Practice with Authentic Language, contains excerpts from published writing. In these exercises, students practice their editing skills by selecting the correct form from alternatives. The next seven appendices offer students a reference guide to irregular verbs; comparatives and superlatives; verb forms; word forms; concise language; a list of vocabulary used in each chapter that comes from the Academic Word List; and commonly used correction symbols. The editing log found in Appendix 9 asks students to record and correct their grammar mistakes in order to become aware of the errors they make most frequently. Appendix 10 is a correlation between the grammar topics presented in *Grammar for Writing 3: An Editing Guide to Writing* and *Understanding and Using English Grammar, Fourth Edition,* and *Focus on Grammar 5, Fourth Edition.* An answer key is available online.

Collaborative and Oral Activities

Grammar for Writing 3: An Editing Guide to Writing lends itself to individual work but is easily adapted to include more communicative activities. Suggestions for collaborative and oral activities include the following:

- After students take the Pretest, ask them to predict the grammar rules for the chapter.

- Have students work with a partner to read the paragraph following the Pretest. Together they can locate the target structures.

- Ask pairs of students to create editing exercises based on their own writing, focusing on the target structures.

- Ask students to submit samples of a target error from their own writing for the development of more exercises.

- Ask students to read their original paragraphs or exercises aloud to a partner to listen for grammatical correctness.

- Ask students to read their partner's writing aloud so that the writers can hear what they have written and check for errors.

- Ask a small group of students to develop a lesson about or an explanation of one grammar topic and present it to the class.

- Ask pairs or small groups to look at pieces of published writing and find examples of the target grammatical structures.

- Have partners, small groups, or the entire class discuss the sample paragraph in the Writing Topics section. Ask them to locate the topic sentence, major and minor supporting points, and concluding sentence. Include a discussion of the outside source used in the paragraph and how it supports the writer's point of view.

- Have partners, small groups, or the entire class participate in a brainstorming session about the writing topics. This will help students develop ideas before they begin the writing assignment.

- Have partners, small groups, or the entire class locate possible support for the writing topics before they begin the writing assignment. Include a discussion of the support that they locate and how it might be included in the students' writing.

- Ask students to work collaboratively on the Writing Topics and submit a collective group paragraph.

- Have a class discussion on the rhetorical features seen in the pieces of published writing in Appendix 1.

- Have partners locate some of the words on the Academic Word List within each chapter (listed in Appendix 7) before they begin writing their own exercises or paragraphs. Include a discussion of how this academic vocabulary is used in the context of the exercise sentence or sample paragraph.

- Ask students to use some of the vocabulary found on the Academic Word List (Appendix 7) as they work collaboratively on developing exercises and writing samples.

To the Student

Grammar for Writing 3: An Editing Guide to Writing presents the rules and practice you need to become a better writer and editor of your own written work. The academic topics, vocabulary, and grammatical structures found in this book are ones that you have become familiar with in many of your college courses and need to include in your own writing. This book has a number of features that will help you accomplish your goal of becoming a fluent and accurate writer.

GRAMMAR TOPICS: The grammar topics in *Grammar for Writing 3: An Editing Guide to Writing* have been chosen based on an analysis of student writing. The grammar points that you will focus on are the ones that advanced writers use in their academic writing. Through practice, you will begin to find, correct, and eventually eliminate common errors in your own writing.

BRIEF EXPLANATIONS: The brief, clear grammar explanations will help you focus on the key points that you need to write and edit your own work successfully. The charts and appendices provide handy tools for quick reference.

STUDENT WRITING: Most exercises are based on academic topics taken from student writing. Therefore, the exercises reflect topics and grammar points that are relevant to college students with an academic focus.

SEQUENCE OF EXERCISES: The pretests help you assess your knowledge of each grammar topic and decide how much practice you need. The subsequent sample paragraphs and exercises in each chapter become progressively more difficult, allowing you to build skills and confidence as you work through them. The last exercise in each chapter gives you the chance to produce and edit your own writing using the grammatical structures that you have been studying.

EXTRA EDITING: In general, when you edit your own writing, you will be looking for various types of errors, not just one type. Therefore, in Chapter 11, you will have additional practice editing for more than one error type in each exercise.

PUBLISHED WRITING: Good writers use other writers' work as models. By analyzing how professional writers use the language, you will improve your own writing. The Practice with Authentic Language exercises in Appendix 1 are drawn from published articles. They will allow you to become more aware of the structures used by professional writers in published material and how to use these structures in your own writing.

EDITING LOG: The editing log found in Appendix 9 will help you focus on the grammar errors that you make most frequently. By recording the grammar mistakes that your teacher finds in your paragraphs and essays, you will begin to see a pattern of errors. Once you know your grammar weaknesses, you can successfully edit for and eliminate them in future writing.

ACADEMIC WORD LIST: The list of academic words found in Appendix 7 is based on the words that are frequently used in college- and university-level writing. These are the words that you will need to know and be able to use to be a successful college student. As you work through the exercises in each chapter, locate the academic words and notice how they are used then practice using some of these words as you write on your own.

Acknowledgments

Many thanks to my colleagues, family, and students, Allison Morgan in particular, who have made *Grammar for Writing 3: An Editing Guide to Writing* possible.

Many more thanks to the Pearson reviewers, marketers, and staff. Most important among these is Marian Wassner, who has taken an extraordinary interest in the development of this book. Always a pleasure to work with, Marian has provided passionate support throughout the many stages of this project. Her professional and knowledgeable guidance have provided the momentum for this book's completion. I cannot thank her enough.

Expressing Present, Past, and Future; Switching Time Frames

GRAMMAR FOCUS

Because verb tense plays such an important role in good writing, it's worth reviewing the different tenses and how they can be used in your writing. Notice that by simply changing the verb tense in the following sentences, the meaning of the sentence changes.

The international economy **is expanding**.   (The present progressive shows an action or situation is occurring at this moment.)
The international economy **has expanded**.   (The present perfect shows an action or situation occurred at an unspecified time in the past.)
The international economy **has been expanding**.   (The present perfect progressive shows an action or situation that began in the past and continues to the present.)

By understanding the subtle differences between verb tenses, you will be able to write with more accuracy.

Pretest

Check your understanding of verb tenses and switching time frames. Put a check (✓) next to the sentences that are correct.

_____ **1.** France is a popular destination for travelers because the French Office of Tourism had promoted France's historical, cultural, and artistic contributions.

_____ **2.** Because professional athletes have been using steroids, the U.S. Congress will have conducted several investigations on this topic over the next several months.

_____ **3.** Dr. Jacques Girard will have published his second book on multiculturalism.

_____ **4.** Scientists have been understanding the process of photosynthesis since the nineteenth century.

_____ **5.** Many people fear that, in the future, states will be entirely responsible for school funding because federal money will have disappeared.

_____ **6.** The federal government had been contributing more to welfare programs before the economy had been taking a downturn last winter.

_____ **7.** The algebra students will have been studying polynomials for an hour by the time the class ends.

_____ **8.** While Jackson Pollock is best known for his abstract paintings, he painted rural American subject matter early in his career.

_____ **9.** Death rates of children in Third World countries had been declining every year since 1960.

_____ **10.** The country two-step dance of the nineteenth century had been slowly changing by the time country dancing became popular again in the late twentieth century.

Notice how the following paragraph uses different verb tenses and switches between time frames. Some of the verbs are underlined. Circle the time word that identifies the tense for each underlined verb.

It seems that we live in a world that is obsessed with celebrities; some people say that we live in a celebrity culture. Centuries ago, religious figures and royalty <u>were</u> the few celebrities of the time, but something <u>has happened</u> during the past decades to increase the number of celebrities and society's obsession with them. A possible reason for this is entertainment television. No fewer than five TV shows <u>have been reporting</u> nightly on celebrities' stories as regular news events. In addition to entertainment TV, there are dozens of celebrity magazines that report every move of famous people. Although similar magazines <u>had existed</u> in past generations, the quantity of this type of magazine <u>grew</u> in the 1980s and <u>has become</u> easily available in every store and newsstand since then. Reality television shows are another possible reason for our obsession with celebrity culture. Everyone believes that it is possible to become famous. Over the past decade, reality television <u>has introduced</u> huge audiences to regular people who have become instant celebrities. Or perhaps the growth of celebrity culture is simply modern society's way of escaping from the real world.

PRESENT TIME

The **simple present** is used for actions or situations that happen now.
To form the simple present, use the base verb or base verb + –s.

USE	EXAMPLE
General truths and facts	Trees **produce** oxygen and filter the air that we breathe.
Habits and routines	Volunteers **work** at polling stations for every election.
Thoughts, feelings, opinions, and preferences	Many citizens **believe** that their taxes are too high. Some groups **feel** that tax reform is necessary. Business owners **prefer** the current tax laws that allow for many deductions.
Discussions of literary and artistic works	In the novel *One Hundred Years of Solitude*, Gabriel Garcia Márquez **blends** fantasy and reality as he **tells** the story of the Buendía family who **establishes** the city of Macondo.

The **present progressive** is used for actions or situations that are in progress right now.
To form the present progressive, use *am/is/are* + present participle.

USE	EXAMPLE
Current actions and states	The world population **is increasing**.
Temporary states and actions	Tessa **is majoring** in chemistry.

The **present perfect** is used for actions or situations that happened in the past but are related to the present.
To form the present perfect, use *have/has* + past participle.

USE	EXAMPLE
Actions happening at an unspecified time in the past, generally the recent past	The university **has** just **decided** to increase tuition by $500 each semester.
Actions beginning in the past and continuing to the present	Professor Johnson **has assigned** homework every day this semester.

NOTE: The present perfect frequently emphasizes a quantity associated with an action.

> *The class* **has read two** *of Steinbeck's novels this semester.*

The **present perfect progressive** emphasizes the continuous nature of an action or situation from the past to the present.

To form the present perfect progressive, use *have/has + been* + present participle.

USE	EXAMPLE
Actions or situations that began in the past and continuously occur to the present	Jiyoung **has been studying** in the United States for six months.

NOTES:

1. The present perfect progressive frequently emphasizes the length of time of an action.

2. Sometimes there is no difference in meaning between the present perfect and the present perfect progressive. This happens with verbs of living and occupation. The following pairs of sentences have the same meaning.

   They **have lived** here for many years.   They **have been living** here for many years.

   He **has worked** in the energy industry since 2008.   He **has been working** in the energy industry since 2008.

Self Check 1

Circle the sentence that uses present time correctly.

1. **(a)** The students have been reading the assignment, but they aren't finished yet.

   (b) The students have read the assignment, but they aren't finished yet.

2. **(a)** The class has just been finishing the final exam.

   (b) The class has just finished the final exam.

3. **(a)** U.S. states hold congressional elections every two years.

   (b) U.S. states are holding congressional elections every two years.

4. **(a)** The Social Security program is currently experiencing budget cuts.

   (b) The Social Security program currently experiences budget cuts.

5. **(a)** The crime rate decreases in most large cities.

   (b) The crime rate has decreased in most large cities.

PAST TIME

The **simple past** is used for actions or situations that happened in the past.

To form the simple past, use the base verb + *–ed* or irregular past forms.

USE	EXAMPLE
Actions or situations with specific past time ending points	Ronald Reagan **died** in 2004.
Past habits and repeated events	The Desert Queen mine **produced** gold until last year.

NOTE: The simple present is used informally to explain past time stories or narratives.

Well, the teacher **tells** *us to take out our books, but my book* **is** *in my car. I* **have to** *leave class to get my book and* **find** *a ticket on my car. I* **am** *really angry at that point and* **decide** *not to return to class.*

The **past progressive** is used for actions or situations that were in progress at a time in the past.

To form the past progressive, use *was/were* + present participle.

USE	EXAMPLE
Actions in progress at a specific past time	The curriculum committee **was meeting** at noon last Wednesday.
Actions interrupted by another past action	The gymnast **was lifting** weights when he pulled his hamstring.
Actions taking place over a period of time	The corn crop **was dying** during the heat wave last summer.

The **past perfect** is used to write about two past actions or situations.

To form the past perfect, use *had* + past participle.

USE	EXAMPLE
A past action that happened before another time or event in the past	Mao Zedong **had established** communism in China before 1950.

The **past perfect progressive** emphasizes the continuous nature of an action or situation that began in the past and continuously occurs until another time in the past.

To form the past perfect progressive, use *had* + *been* + present participle.

USE	EXAMPLE
A past action that happens continuously until another past time or action	By 8:00 A.M., the children **had been sleeping** for ten hours.
A past action that happens continuously until it is interrupted by another past action	Elena and Diana **had been studying** until the library closed at midnight.

Self Check 2

Circle the sentence that uses past time correctly.

1. **(a)** It was obvious that the model had been dieting because she was so thin.

   (b) It was obvious that the model dieted because she was so thin.

2. **(a)** By 1992 the poet had composed poetry for several presidential inaugurations.

   (b) By 1992 the poet was composing poetry for several presidential inaugurations.

3. **(a)** Humans had first landed on the moon in 1969.

   (b) Humans first landed on the moon in 1969.

4. **(a)** Jonas Salk was performing an experiment when he discovered the polio vaccine.

   (b) Jonas Salk performed an experiment when he discovered the polio vaccine.

5. **(a)** Dr. Tomi had been majoring in chemistry before he changed to computer science.

   (b) Dr. Tomi majored in chemistry before he had changed to computer science.

FUTURE TIME

The **simple future** is used for actions or situations that will happen in the future.

To form the simple future, use *will* + base verb.

USE	EXAMPLE
Scheduled events and probable future actions	The World Trade Organization **will hold** its annual meeting next month. The Chinese manufacturing industry **will grow** in the next decades.
Offers and promises	Many organizations **will donate** thousands of dollars to end poverty in Africa.
Quick decisions	A: I need a ride to the bus stop. B: I**'ll take** you.

***Be going to* + verb** is also used for actions or situations that will happen in the future; however, there is more certainty with *be going to* than with *will*.

To form the future with *be going to*, use *am/is/are* + *going to* + base verb.

USE	EXAMPLE
Planned events that will happen soon	The intern **is going to present** her research project tomorrow.
Predictions	The governor believes that the state assembly **is going to pass** the bill.

The **future progressive** emphasizes the continuous nature of actions or situations that will be in progress in the future.

To form the future progressive, use *will* + *be* + present participle.

USE	EXAMPLE
A future action that will begin soon and continue for a period of time	The class **will be reviewing** for finals all of next week.

The **future perfect** is used for actions or situations that will happen before another future time.

To form the future perfect, use *will* + *have* + past participle.

USE	EXAMPLE
Two future events when one happens before the other	By the end of next year, Dennis **will have graduated** from medical school. However, he **will not have finished** his medical residency before he graduates.

The **future perfect progressive** emphasizes the continuous nature of an action or situation that will be in progress before a specific time in the future.

To form the future perfect progressive, use *will* + *have* + *been* + present participle.

USE	EXAMPLE
A future event that will be happening continuously before another future event or time	The airline industry **will have been serving** commercial passengers for 100 years by the end of next year. By the time I finish my Ph.D. dissertation, I **will have been working** on it for five years.

The **simple present** can also be used for future actions or situations.

To form the future with the simple present, use the base verb or base verb + –*s*.

USE	EXAMPLE
Scheduled or expected events	The debate tournament **begins** next weekend.
Dependent clauses with adverbs of time	After the bride and groom **finish** the wedding ceremony, the guests will go to the reception.

The **present progressive** can also be used for future actions or situations, except for predictions or offers.

To form the future with the present progressive, use *am/is/are* + present participle.

USE	EXAMPLE
Previously arranged future events	The Olympic Committee **is choosing** the site of the next winter games in a few months.

WRITING TIP

You have just reviewed the twelve verb tenses in English; however, only six of the tenses are used frequently. These tenses include the simple present, present progressive, present perfect, simple past, past progressive, and future. Although it is important to understand and use all twelve tenses, spend most of your time focusing on the six most commonly used tenses.

Circle the sentence that uses future time correctly.

1. (a) Strict gun control laws will have been saving lives for two decades by 2020.

(b) Strict gun control laws will be saving lives for two decades by 2020.

2. (a) The fast-food chains will have cut the fat in their food by 50 percent in three years.

(b) The fast-food chains will have been cutting the fat in their food by 50 percent in three years.

3. (a) A: Who can help me with my calculus homework? B: I'm going to help you later today.

(b) A: Who can help me with my calculus homework? B: I'll help you later today.

4. (a) Some educators believe that every student needs to speak a foreign language someday.

(b) Some educators believe that every student will need to speak a foreign language someday.

5. (a) The weather is hot and humid in Hawaii tomorrow.

(b) The weather is going to be hot and humid in Hawaii tomorrow.

WRITING WITHIN TIME FRAMES

The same time frames generally occur together within a piece of writing. For example, if you begin writing in the present tense, you will probably remain within the present and future time frames. Notice how the following passage uses only present time and future time.

For-profit universities **enroll** *many students who* **work** *full-time and* **go** *to school in the evening. Their enrollment has increased substantially over the past decade. However, these universities will experience hardships if businesses stop paying tuition fees for their employees to return to school.*

BEFORE THE PRIMARY TIME: PRESENT PERFECT OR PRESENT PERFECT PROGRESSIVE	PRIMARY TIME: SIMPLE PRESENT	AFTER THE PRIMARY TIME: SIMPLE FUTURE OR FUTURE PROGRESSIVE
Their enrollment **has increased** substantially over the past decade.	For-profit universities **enroll** many students who **work** full-time and **go** to school in the evening.	However, these universities **will experience** hardships if businesses stop paying tuition fees for their employees to return to school.

A similar pattern of tenses is seen in pieces of writing that use the past time frames. If you are writing in the past, you will probably remain within the past time frames. Notice how the passage on page 9 uses only past time.

Enrollment in for-profit universities **began** *to rise in the first few years of the twenty-first century. Before the increase in for-profits, traditional public and private universities* **had been enrolling** *most college-bound students. After several years of quick growth in enrollments, for-profit colleges* **were facing** *complaints from students about poor quality education, which* **led** *to investigations by the government.*

BEFORE THE PRIMARY TIME: PAST PERFECT OR PAST PERFECT PROGRESSIVE	PRIMARY TIME: SIMPLE PAST	AFTER THE PRIMARY TIME: SIMPLE PAST AND PAST PROGRESSIVE
Before the increase in for-profits, traditional public and private universities **had been enrolling** most college-bound students.	Enrollment in for-profit universities **began** to rise in the first few years of the twenty-first century.	After several years of quick growth in enrollments, for-profit colleges **were facing** complaints from students about poor quality education, which **led** to investigations by the government.

Staying within the same general time frame is also important in a piece of writing that is about the future. When you begin writing in the future tense, you will generally remain within the future time frame. Notice how the following passage uses only future time.

Large segments of the population **will continue** *to need alternatives to traditional public and private universities that* **are going to remain** *popular with traditional college students. Typically students at for-profit universities* **will have experienced** *job stagnation or unemployment before returning to school. Nontraditional universities such as for-profits* **will provide** *the flexibility necessary for this group of students.*

BEFORE THE PRIMARY TIME: FUTURE PERFECT OR FUTURE PERFECT PROGRESSIVE	PRIMARY TIME: SIMPLE FUTURE OR *BE GOING TO*	AFTER THE PRIMARY TIME: SIMPLE FUTURE OR *BE GOING TO*
Typically students at for-profit universities **will have experienced** job stagnation or unemployment before returning to school.	Large segments of the population **will continue** to need alternatives to traditional public and private universities that **are going to remain** popular with traditional college students.	Nontraditional universities such as for-profits **will provide** the flexibility necessary for this group of students.

SWITCHING BETWEEN TIME FRAMES

Using Time Words

You will want to keep the previous description of time frames in mind as you write a paragraph, essay, or longer piece of writing. Staying within one time frame helps the flow of a piece of writing. However, switching between present, past, and future time frames is also necessary. This can be done by adding a time word to let the reader know that the time frame is changing. Notice how the following passage begins in the present time frame, switches to the past, and then to the future; each time the writer switches time frames, a time word is added to announce the change.

*For-profit universities enroll many students who work full-time and go to school in the evening. Their enrollment has increased substantially **over the past decade**. Enrollment in for-profit universities began to rise **in the first few years of the twenty-first century**. Before the increase in for-profits, traditional public and private universities had been enrolling most college-bound students. **In the future**, large segments of the population will continue to need alternatives to traditional public and private universities. Therefore, these institutions must be regulated **today** so that they will be able to provide quality education for students **in the coming decades**.*

Using No Time Words

Time frames within a piece of writing may change without the use of time words. This frequently occurs when the writer is moving from a general topic to specific support of the topic. Notice how the following passage uses the present time to introduce the topic and switches to the past time to provide support or specific examples.

*The enrollment in for-profit universities **is increasing** as workers **look** for ways to improve their job prospects in an economy that **has been shrinking**. This can be seen in the for-profits' enrollments, which **grew** approximately 300 percent. There **were** approximately 2,000 for-profit universities that **enrolled** nearly 2 million students compared to 800 for-profit universities that **had enrolled** only 700,000 students a few years earlier.*

Writers can also begin in the past time and switch to the present. Notice how the following passage begins by introducing a specific example from the past and then comments on the topic by using the present time.

*In 2009 for-profit universities **enrolled** 10 percent of higher education students but **received** 24 percent of public funds that **paid** for their tuition. Although these universities **are** private businesses, much of their growth **has been funded** by federal student aid. This **is raising** alarm within the government, as much of the student loan money **is not repaid** and there **is** a low graduation rate among students at for-profit universities.*

WRITING TIP

Use the reading that you do in your other classes or in your free time to help with your writing. Notice how writers use verb tenses and switch from one time frame to another. By analyzing others' writing, you will be improving your own.[1]

---

[1] For more information about patterns of tenses and time frames in longer pieces of writing, see Bull, William. *Time, Tense, and the Verb: A Study in Theoretical and Applied Linguistics, with Particular Application to Spanish.* Berkeley and Los Angeles: The University of California Press, 1960.

EDITING PRACTICE

1. *Put a check (✓) next to the sentences that use verb tenses and time frames correctly. Correct the sentences that have errors. There may be more than one way to correct some errors.*

_____ **1.** By the end of the twenty-first century, written forms of poetry will exist for over 1,000 years.

_____ **2.** When the earth's plates ram into each other, the enormous pressure creates mountain ranges.

_____ **3.** As the earth compacts clay sediment, the clay will have eventually turned into slate.

_____ **4.** Andrew Jackson, the seventh president of the United States, believed that the banking system was corrupt and worked only to make the rich richer.

_____ **5.** Prior to the Civil War, southern leaders had been advocating for the South to separate from the United States.

_____ **6.** Many early settlers who came to America were searching for a utopian society that has not existed before.

_____ **7.** Doctors have not been finding a reliable method to control glucose levels in diabetes patients yet.

_____ **8.** By the time Jennifer gets her Ph.D., she will have been studying for almost ten years.

_____ **9.** The current president will have left the Oval Office moments before the new president takes over the position.

_____ **10.** As the use of tanning beds has increased, doctors have been seeing an increase in skin cancer cases.

_____ **11.** As ocean levels rise, island nations such as Japan, Indonesia, and the Philippines will be push for strong climate change agreements between countries.

_____ **12.** It is controversial that some countries now begin to grow crops for biofuel rather than for food to feed their hungry populations.

2. *Read the following paragraph. Complete the paragraph with the correct verb tense.*

Because of the current obesity epidemic among our children, a growing

number of special-interest groups _____
                                    1. will fight / are fighting

for the integration of yoga into the daily or weekly curriculum of

elementary schools. They _____ to
                          2. were trying / have been trying

stress the importance of training children in yoga from an early age in order to make the children aware of their bodies and minds before

they _____ unhealthy habits that are
          3. develop / will develop

difficult to break later in life. Also, they note that children's lack of activity

_____ widespread in today's society,
          4. became / has become

and the integration of yoga _____ in
                                  5. will result / will have resulted

more exercise. In theory, by the time these children are adults, their

early exposure to exercise _____ to
                                6. is leading / will have led

a healthy lifestyle. By simply moving the desks in a classroom, the

children _____ the room into a yoga
          7. transformed / will be transforming

studio where they can relax and release some of their energy. Preliminary

research on children who _____
                              8. had been practicing / will be practicing

yoga during the school day showed that they had a better ability to

focus, which _____ their learning
                9. increased / will have increased

capability. These results are furthering the belief that children who

_____ exercise to relieve their stress and
          10. lack / lacked

energy are not happy children, and, as the saying goes, healthy children are

happy children.

3. *In the following paragraph, the underlined verbs are not correct. Write the correct tense above each underlined verb. There may be more than one way to correct some errors.*

Historians <u>have been study</u> George Washington since his death in 1799.
                      1

Their interest includes not only his life and accomplishments but also his

plantation home, Mount Vernon. In 1999, excavation of Mount Vernon

<u>had begun</u> with the goal of finding the remains of Washington's distillery.
  2

Historians and scientists were hoping to find information about both

Washington and the distillery industry during the late eighteenth century. In addition, a replica of the distillery was to be recreated for tourists to view. Previous studies of Mt. Vernon <u>were locating</u> the position of the distillery, **3** but the 1999 excavation uncovered several notable features. Where scientists <u>had excavating</u> just below the surface, they found a brick drain, a trench **4** of preserved wood, and some large foundation stones. They additionally <u>founded</u> a layer of brick flooring, an unusual feature in an era when wood **5** floors <u>were being</u> the norm. Stone or brick floors had become a necessity in **6** distilleries because of the heat used to turn grain into alcohol. Washington <u>had been mentioning</u> many of these features in journals that he wrote in **7** daily. What was not found during the excavation was equally interesting. Records from old insurance documents <u>were stating</u> that the distillery was **8** 75 by 30 feet, but the newly excavated foundation was only 60 by 30 feet. Researchers interestingly concluded that neighbors <u>had took</u> part of **9** the distillery's floor to use as building materials for themselves. Although archeologists are still conducting research at the site of Washington's distillery, the replica was completed in 2006. Since then tourists <u>has been visiting</u> the distillery on their trips to Mount Vernon. **10**

4. *The following paragraphs have ten verb tense errors. Find and correct the errors. There may be more than one way to correct some errors.*

Fraternities and sororities are popular social organizations for undergraduates on many college campuses. In addition to social activities, these organizations provided academic support as well as residential and dining facilities. Fraternities and sororities will have received both praise and criticism for their actions during the past years.

One of the positive features of fraternities and sororities is their philanthropy. Before I was an undergraduate, my sorority has partnered with St. Jude Children's Hospital, and during the four years before I graduated, we had been working together to help children at St. Jude. The national organization of my sorority will have been raising $10 million for St. Jude within the next three years. Throughout the past several years, all of the fraternities and sororities on my campus are competing against each other to raise the most money for their philanthropies. In contrast to their charitable work, fraternities and sororities have received criticism for their dangerous hazing rituals. Hazing, making new members do silly or dangerous actions as one of the requirements to join the organization, occurs in fraternities and sororities since they were established several hundred years ago. However, hazing has been illegal in most states in the United States because it has resulted in numerous injuries and even deaths. Because of several hazing incidents at my university three years ago, the university kicks two fraternities off campus, and they didn't return for ten years. By the time the university allows them back on campus, the other fraternities have grown, which will make it difficult for the two disgraced fraternities to reestablish themselves on campus. Like many social organizations, fraternities and sororities can be both praised and criticized; members can only hope that their organization's positive work outweighs their negative reputations.

WRITING TOPICS

Most academic essays and research papers require an introduction with a strong thesis statement. The body paragraphs following the introduction support the thesis with references to outside sources. These outside sources might be summarized, quoted, or paraphrased. Notice how the following body paragraph, which was taken from a longer piece of writing, includes a topic sentence, a body with support from outside sources, and a concluding sentence. Use this paragraph as a model when you write about one of the following topics.

Study the use of verb tenses in the following student paragraph. Put a check in the margin of your book where you notice a switch in time frames. Why do you think the writer made this change?

Our beliefs about class, clothing, and appearance influence many decisions that we make in our daily lives. With this in mind, the teacher profiled in Cindy Silvester's article "Barbie Doll" sought to teach a lesson on stereotyping to her first- through third-grade students. In the article published in *The Times Educational Supplement*, Silvester described a lesson in which the teacher showed her students several Barbie and Ken dolls that were dressed shabbily and others that were dressed nicely.[1]  The teacher explained to Silvester that the students assigned character traits to each of the differently dressed dolls. Although the students were told a doll's character does not depend on its clothing, the teacher noted that every year she teaches this lesson, the students assign positive and negative traits to the dolls that directly correspond to the doll's clothing. The follow-up discussion eventually led these six- to nine-year-olds to the idea that even though people may look different on the outside, outward appearances do not define who a person is. While this news story didn't attract national attention, it made an important point: The lessons that society teaches its children about class, clothing, and appearance will have an effect on its future.

Choose one of the topics below and write at least one paragraph. Find an outside source to support the ideas that you present in your writing. Use a variety of verb tenses and time frames. After you complete your first draft, concentrate on editing your work. Keep in mind the editing practice from this chapter.

1. Write about the qualities that make a hero. Provide one or more examples of real-life heroes that exemplify the qualities that make a person heroic.

2. What is the most important news story this year? Explain why this story is so important.

Go to page 165 for more practice with verb tenses and time shifts.

....

[1] Silvester, Cindy. "Barbie Doll," *TES Connect*, May 11, 2007. http://www.tes.co.uk/article.aspx?storycode=2382838.

2 The Passive Voice and Participial Adjectives

GRAMMAR FOCUS

While forming the passive voice (*be* + past participle) is not a problem for most advanced writers, using it appropriately may be more difficult. The passive voice can occur quite frequently; therefore, understanding when to use it and which verbs can form the passive are important for advanced writers. Additionally, there are different forms of passive sentences, and they have different purposes. Notice how the following two sentences are both passive, but one indicates an action while the other indicates a condition.

| DYNAMIC PASSIVE | Four different blood groups **were discovered** by Karl Landsteiner in 1901. |
| STATIVE PASSIVE | The four blood groups **were composed of** A, B, AB, and O. |

This chapter will help you distinguish between these different forms and compose sentences that use the passive voice appropriately.

Pretest

Check your understanding of the passive voice. Put a check (✓) next to the sentences that are correct.

_____ **1.** The earthquake got felt across the entire chain of islands.

_____ **2.** Medication is required daily for those with high blood pressure.

_____ **3.** New cars have being created with special sensors that can detect when the driver is falling asleep.

_____ **4.** The sale and consumption of alcohol had been prohibited for thirteen years by the Eighteenth Amendment until it was repealed in 1933.

_____ **5.** The author's new book will have been edited before it gets published next year.

_____ **6.** Frederic Auguste Bartholdi had his design of the Statue of Liberty patented in 1879.

_____ **7.** The criminal avoided being arrest until all his wealth was hidden in a foreign bank account.

_____ **8.** All facilities in the complex are going to be maintaining by the landlord.

_____ **9.** The city of Kobe in Japan was become famous for its very expensive and tender beef.

_____ **10.** Many architecture students are interesting in sustainable design.

Notice how the following paragraph uses the passive voice. Circle the six verbs that are in the passive voice.

Many scholars view the Trail of Tears in the 1830s as the most disturbing event of President Andrew Jackson's presidency. This event began when the Indian Removal Act was passed in 1830. It forced Native Americans to be moved from their eastern homelands to western lands. After several legal battles, Jackson convinced some Cherokee Indians to sign a treaty that permitted the government to move them west; however, it was discovered that the Cherokee signers were not allowed to review this document. Over 15,000 Cherokees protested the government's action, but their petition was ignored by the U.S. government. Instead, federal troops forced them to march west in an action that killed nearly 5,000 Cherokees and that today is known as the Trail of Tears.

FORMING THE PASSIVE VOICE

1. The passive voice is formed with the verb *be* + past participle. The *be* verb always indicates the tense and must agree with the subject.

VERB TENSE FORMING THE PASSIVE VOICE	ACTIVE	PASSIVE
Simple Present *am/is/are* + past participle	The new requirement **forces** students to graduate within four years.	Because of the new requirement, students **are forced** to graduate within four years.
Present Progressive *am/is/are* + *being* + past participle	The Transportation Safety Board **is conducting** full body searches at all airports.	Full body searches **are being conducted** by the Transportation Safety Board at all airports.
Present Perfect *has/have* + *been* + past participle	According to death penalty opponents, the death penalty **has not deterred** crime.	According to death penalty opponents, crime **has not been deterred** by the death penalty.
Simple Past *was/were* + past participle	Alexander Fleming **discovered** penicillin in 1928.	Penicillin **was discovered** by Alexander Fleming in 1928.
Past Progressive *was/were* + *being* + past participle	The class **was not reading** any of Shakespeare's comedies last semester.	Shakespeare's comedies **were not being read** by the class last semester.
Past Perfect *had* + *been* + past participle	Predators **had threatened** the existence of the Island Fox before the Environmental Protection Agency placed it on the endangered species list.	The existence of the Island Fox **had been threatened** by predators before the Environmental Protection Agency placed it on the endangered species list.
Simple Future *will* + *be* + past participle	Pharmaceutical companies **will not improve** antiaging treatments in the coming years.	Antiaging treatments **will not be improved** by pharmaceutical companies in the coming years.
be + *going to* + verb *am/is/are* + *going to* + *be* + past participle	Hospitals and medical offices **are going to computerize** all medical records.	All medical records **are going to be computerized** by hospitals and medical offices.
Future Perfect *will* + *have* + *been* + past participle	The president **will have signed** legislation to change health care before he leaves office.	Legislation to change health care **will have been signed** by the president before he leaves office.

NOTE: The passive forms of the present perfect progressive, past perfect progressive, and future perfect progressive are very rarely used and are not covered in this book.

2. Present and past time modals can be used in the passive voice.

MODALS FORMING THE PASSIVE VOICE	ACTIVE	PASSIVE
Present and future modals modal + *be* + past participle	The government **should not ban** mining because this industry provides many jobs in poor regions.	Mining **should not be banned** by the government because this industry provides many jobs in poor regions.
Past modals modal + *have been* + past participle	Cloud seeding **may have caused** the good weather during the Beijing Olympic Games.	The good weather during the Beijing Olympic Games **may have been caused** by cloud seeding.

NOTE: The passive voice generally occurs with modals that show:

Ability:	Coffee **can be grown** best within the bean belt, the region between the Topics of Cancer and Capricorn.
Possibility:	The eclipse **could be seen** in the southern hemisphere.
Near Certainty:	He **must have been injured** when his car rolled over in the accident.
Suggestions:	Schools **should be supported** by donations from their local communities.

3. Infinitives and gerunds can be used in the passive voice.

VERB + INFINITIVE OR GERUND FORMING THE PASSIVE VOICE	PASSIVE
verb + infinitive verb + *to be* + past participle For example, *agree, expect, learn,* and *refuse*	The defendant didn't **agree to be taken** to court in handcuffs. He **expected to be treated** as innocent until proven guilty.
verb + gerund verb + *being* + past participle For example, *avoid, keep, miss,* and *permit*	Although they may deny it, celebrities **miss being followed** by the paparazzi. They **keep being photographed** in locations that are known as paparazzi hangouts.

Self Check 1

Circle the sentence that forms the passive voice correctly.

1. (a) Meals should be eating slowly so that we have time to feel full and do not overeat.

   (b) Meals should be eaten slowly so that we have time to feel full and do not overeat.

2. (a) Background actors are used only once or twice per season in most TV shows.

   (b) Background actors are use only once or twice per season in most TV shows.

3. (a) Some members of the military learn to be treating as property rather than as individuals.

(b) Some members of the military learn to be treated as property rather than as individuals.

4. (a) The verdict will have been decided by the time the jurors finish their deliberations.

(b) The verdict will have being decided by the time the jurors finish their deliberations.

5. (a) George Washington had being asked to run for a third term as president, but he refused.

(b) George Washington had been asked to run for a third term as president, but he refused.

USING THE PASSIVE VOICE

1. The passive voice is often used in the following situations:

- the person or thing doing the action (the agent) is obvious, unknown, or unimportant.

    The Treaty of Versailles **was signed** *June 28, 1919, at the end of World War I.*

- you don't want to mention the person doing the action or you want to be discrete.

    The car **was being driven** *recklessly.*

- you want to emphasize the receiver of the action or the result of the action.

    A child **should be taught** *a second or third language at a young age.*

    A second or third language **can be learned** *easily at a young age.*

- you are describing a process.

    The essay topic **is introduced** *in class before it* **is researched** *by the students.*

    Next, several drafts **are written**, *and finally the last draft* **is turned in**.

- you want your writing to sound objective.

    It **is believed** *that the police chief took bribes from people in the community.*

- you introduce new information in the first sentence with the active voice and expand on that information in the following sentence with the passive voice. This use of the passive voice can help the flow of ideas within a piece of writing.

    The students will write five papers this semester. The papers **are going to be based** *on several short stories.*

    (In the first sentence, *five papers* represent new information; in the second sentence, they are familiar and can be explained more completely.)

    The mayor presented his ideas on balancing the city budget. His ideas **were supported** *by most of the community.*

    (In the first sentence, *his ideas* represent new information; in the second sentence, they are familiar and can be explained more completely.)

Although all good writing includes both the active and passive voice, writers generally prefer the active voice unless one of the six situations just explained is present. Always look carefully at the passive sentences in your writing to make sure that there might not be a better way of writing the same information in the active voice.

2. Most passive sentences in English do not include a *by* phrase that states who the agent is. The *by* phrase should be included in a passive sentence only if it contains important information, such as when:

- the agent is new information.

  Potatoes **were** *first* **introduced** *in Europe by the Spanish.*

- the agent is an important or famous person who should be identified by his or her proper name.

  The Great Irish Potato Famine **was written about** *by Leon Uris and George Bernard Shaw.*

- the agent is inanimate (not a person).

  Potato sales **have been strengthened** *by the consumption of French fries in fast-food restaurants.*

3. The passive voice can be formed only with transitive verbs (verbs that can have a direct object). Intransitive verbs (verbs that cannot have a direct object) cannot be passive. The following is a list of some commonly-used intransitive verbs. Do not use these verbs in the passive voice.

arrive	belong	(dis)agree	go	remain	sleep
be	come	(dis)appear	happen	rise	stay
become	die	exist	occur	seem	work

WRITING TIP

Develop a personal dictionary that lists the verbs you frequently use. Classify the verbs into two categories: verbs that can be active and passive and verbs that cannot be passive.

Active and passive: *bring, deny, give, offer, owe, send, show, teach, etc.*

Not passive: *be, happen, have, seem, etc.*

4. The passive voice can be formed with *get* as well as *be*.

- *Get* is generally more informal and conversational than *be* in passive sentences.

  Formal: *Historically, women* **have been paid** *less than men.*

  More informal: *Historically, women* **have gotten paid** *less than men.*

- *Get* usually does not have an agent, but *be* frequently does.

  Agent: *Sometimes teenagers* **may be convinced** *by their peers to smoke cigarettes.*

  No agent: *Teenagers may* **get convinced** *to participate in dangerous activities.*

- *Get* frequently expresses a process or action whereas *be* often expresses a state.

  State: *Nearly 52 percent of the United States population* **is married**.

  Process: *Over 2 million people* **got married** *last year in the United States.*

- *Get* implies that the subject has involvement in the action while *be* shows little or no involvement by the subject. Therefore, the subject of most passive sentences that use *get* is human.

  No involvement by the subject

  The faculty **are dressed** *in their graduation regalia.*

  Involvement by the subject

  The children **got dressed** *in their Halloween costumes.*

NOTE: When *get* is used in the passive voice, it cannot be used as the auxiliary verb in questions and negative statements. *Do* must be used as the auxiliary.

get passive (affirmative statement)

The Democratic candidate **got elected** *to office.*

get passive (question)

Did *the Democratic candidate* **get elected** *to office?*

get passive (negative statement)

The Democratic candidate **did not get elected** *to office.*

5. The passive voice can also be formed with *have*. *Have* and *get* passives are similar in meaning. However, *have* passives must include an object that is placed between *have* and the past participle.

   Passive with *have* (have + object + past participle)

   Numerous companies **have had** *their products* **manufactured** *in China since the late twentieth century. They* **have** *this* **done** *to cut costs.*

   Passive with *be*

   Products from numerous companies **have been manufactured** *in China since the late twentieth century. This* **is done** *to cut costs.*

   Passive with *get*

   Products from numerous companies **have gotten manufactured** *in China since the late twentieth century. This* **gets done** *to cut costs.*

6. Passive verbs that describe a situation are called stative passives. Stative passives are formed with *be* + past participle, but they do not have *by* phrases because stative passives are used to describe a situation or state rather than to show an action. Stative passives are often followed by a preposition other than *by*.

   In most research papers, statistics **may be found** *inside tables and graphs.*

   Machu Picchu **is located** *at approximately 8,000 feet in the mountains of Peru.*

   Traditional kimonos **are made** *of silk and satin.*

Some academic verbs are commonly used as stative passives.

call	*Children born after World War II **are called** Baby Boomers.*
compose of	*Water **is composed of** hydrogen and oxygen.*
consider	*Republican appointees to the Supreme Court **are considered** the most conservative justices on the Supreme Court.*
cover with	*About 70 percent of the earth's surface **is covered with** water.*
divide into	*The United States government **is divided into** three parts: the executive, legislative, and judicial branches.*
find	*Great white sharks **have been found** in every ocean of the world.*
know for/as	*Albert Einstein **is known for** the theory of relativity. (= is remembered for)*
	*The year 1905 **is known as** Albert Einstein's "Miracle Year." (= is named or called)*
locate	*Nepal **is located** high in the Himalayan Mountains.*
make up of	*The London Underground **is made up of** 270 stations and 250 miles of track.*
use	*The passive voice **is** often **used** to describe a scientific process.*

Self Check 2

Circle the sentence that uses the passive voice correctly.

1. **(a)** The infant was dressed in a long white gown for her baptism.

   (b) The infant got dressed in a long white gown for her baptism.

2. **(a)** Olive oil has been found to be beneficial for healthy hair and skin.

   (b) Olive oil has been found by people to be beneficial for healthy hair and skin.

3. **(a)** The existence of the Holy Grail has debated by many historians.

   (b) The existence of the Holy Grail has been debated by many historians.

4. **(a)** In the seventeenth and eighteenth centuries, the wealthy had their clothing made by European designers.

   (b) In the seventeenth and eighteenth centuries, the wealthy had made their clothing by European designers.

5. **(a)** Over 500 species of bacteria exist in the human digestive tract.

   (b) Over 500 species of bacteria are existed in the human digestive tract.

PARTICIPIAL ADJECTIVES

Participial adjectives are adjectives that are formed from verbs and used like adjectives. These adjectives generally show emotions such as disappointment, interest, or boredom. Participial adjectives may be active or passive.

1. Passive participial adjectives communicate a passive meaning. A passive participial adjective describes an existing situation or state just like a stative passive.

    *The **depressed** patients tried counseling before taking medication.*

    • Passive participial adjectives end in *–ed/–en*.

    *The **confused** students asked many questions.*

    *A **broken** window can be dangerous.*

    • Passive participial adjectives can form passive sentences.

    *The students **have been confused** since the first day of class.*

    *The window **was broken** by the children who were throwing balls.*

    • Passive participial adjectives generally describe something living.

    ***Annoyed citizens** voted in large numbers during the last election.*

    *A **disappointed child** cried during the birthday party.*

    • Passive participial adjectives describe temporary emotions or states.

    *The class **was disappointed** when the teacher didn't return the exams promptly.*

2. Active participial adjectives communicate an active meaning. An active participial adjective modifies a noun that does something.

    *The **challenging** course forced the students to study a lot.*

    • Active participial adjectives end in *–ing*.

    ***Confusing** formulas cause a lot of problems for math students.*

    *An **amusing** movie is always more popular than a dramatic one.*

    • Active participial adjectives can be used in active sentences.

    *The algebra and geometry formulas **were confusing** to the math students.*

    *Some movies can be **amusing** for both children and adults.*

    • Active participial adjectives generally describe something that is not living.

    ***Annoying noises** kept us awake last night.*

    ***Disappointing test scores** made some students drop the class.*

3. Compare how active and passive meanings are communicated in the following sentences.

Passive verb:	*The stockholders **were disappointed** by the company's profits.*
Passive adjective:	*The **disappointed** stockholders sold their shares in the company.*
Active verb:	*The company's profits **disappointed** the stockholders.*
Active adjective:	*The **disappointing** profits caused the stockholders to sell their shares.*
	*The company's profits were **disappointing**, so the stockholders sold their shares.*

4. The following is a list of some commonly-used participial adjectives. Study these carefully to avoid making mistakes in their use.

amazed/amazing	excited/exciting	interested/interesting
annoyed/annoying	exhausted/exhausting	satisfied/satisfying
bored/boring	fascinated/fascinating	shocked/shocking
damaged/demanding	frightened/frightening	surprised/surprising
depressed/depressing	frozen/freezing	terrified/terrifying
disappointed/disappointing	frustrated/frustrating	tired/tiring
embarrassed/embarrassing	grown/growing	

*The **annoying** commercials made the **annoyed** viewers turn off the TV.*

*The **frightened** survivors knew that there would be more **frightening** earthquakes.*

NOTE: Some participial adjectives are generally in the passive form (*abandoned, balanced, crowded, given, required, spoiled, stolen*), while others are generally in the active form (*flying, following, leading, sleeping*). Some participial adjectives are irregular (*bothered/bothersome, delighted/delightful, scared/scary, wasted/wasteful*).

Self Check 3

Circle the sentence that uses the correct participial adjective.

1. (a) The chemistry lab experiments are long and tiring.

   (b) The chemistry lab experiments are long and tired.

2. (a) The employees felt satisfied after their pay raise.

   (b) The employees felt satisfying after their pay raise.

3. (a) The abandoning building attracts crime.

   (b) The abandoned building attracts crime.

4. (a) Wasting water usage hurts the environment.

   (b) Wasteful water usage hurts the environment.

5. (a) The politician's comments were shocked.

   (b) The politician's comments were shocking.

EDITING PRACTICE

1. *Put a check (✓) next to the sentences that use the passive voice correctly. Correct the sentences that have errors.*

_____ **1.** Many veterans have been diagnosed with post-traumatic stress disorder after witnessing the horrors of war.

_____ **2.** Perfectly preserved artifacts were not expected to be find in the ruins of Pompeii.

_____ **3.** Bottled water, canned foods, and other supplies were being buying in record numbers during the scare at the turn of the millennium.

_____ **4.** Tooth decay caused by acid-producing bacteria.

_____ **5.** More couples got divorced last year than in any previous years.

_____ **6.** Soda and junk food were place on the list of banned foods in many school cafeterias because of new nutrition regulations.

_____ **7.** Frozen food was considered revolutionary in 1923 when Clarence Birdseye invented it.

_____ **8.** Because there are so many pets without homes, most pet owners should have their pets spayed or neutered.

_____ **9.** The earliest navigation was achieved with the use of the stars as markers by people.

_____ **10.** Overnight parking in the downtown area is not allow without a parking permit.

_____ **11.** In the future, acrylic paints are going to be replaced by computer graphics for movie and stage productions.

_____ **12.** Photographs of the far side of Pluto will have been taking by the end of the next decade.

2. *Read the following paragraph. Complete the paragraph with the correct form of the verb or adjective.*

In professional theater, one of the most important jobs

that _____ is the prop master.
    1. has being overlooked / has been overlooked

The prop master is responsible for all theatrical property,

which _____ as props. Props
        2. is known / knows

include any object that _____
            3. is used / is using

on stage by an actor during a theatrical production.

Small props _____
        4. are call / are called

hand props, while larger props might include

objects such as furniture, bicycles, or ladders. The

prop master _____
        5. must locate / must be located

all of the objects for a production. These objects

_____. Because
6. can be rented, bought, borrowed, or built / can rent, buy, borrow, or build

most productions generally have very small budgets, the prop master

_____ for his or her resourcefulness in
      7. must be known / must know

making the show appear real but not going over budget. For example,

in the show *Noises Off!* an ax _____
                       8. is needed / is needing

in one scene of the play. Due to safety concerns, the actors

_____ to use a real ax, so the prop master
   9. are not allowed / did not get allowed

has to find a realistic, cost-effective substitute. In the original production

of this show in 2008, it _____ by the
           10. had been decided / had been decide

prop master to use scrap materials in the theater shop to create the

_____ ax. In all theater productions, it is a
     11. frightening / frightened

_____ job to take an empty stage and bring
    12. challenged / challenging

it to life, but this is what a good prop master must do.

3. *In the following paragraph, the underlined verbs and adjectives are not correct. Write the correct form of each underlined verb or adjective above the underlined word(s).*

    In 1943, Abraham Maslow proposed a theory in psychology that

describes the five stages of human growth: physiological, safety, love, esteem,

and self-actualization. If one studies Maslow's Hierarchy of Needs, it

<u>can be see</u> that a child's performance in school <u>will be affecting</u> by his or
  1   2

her home environment. Before children can express creativity and curiosity

at school, the first four levels <u>must to be satisfied</u>. Children who come
                                    3

from impoverished backgrounds may find it difficult to satisfy their

first-level needs, which include food, water, and sleep. Some schools

<u>have had started breakfast programs</u> to help compensate for this deficiency,
                    4

but limited funding has reduced these programs. After physiological needs,

Maslow says it is necessary to satisfy safety needs. Poor neighborhoods

<u>tend to be locate</u> in areas where it is not safe for young people to grow up.
    5

Schools have little control over this situation but feel the effects if children

come to school feeling unsafe and <u>frightening</u>. According to Maslow, the
                                      6

next level that <u>has to achieve</u> is the child's need for love from both peers
                   7

and parents. Poor children <u>can discriminate</u> against by their peers because
                                8

of their shabby appearance or the neighborhood where they live. If a poor

child <u>is picking on</u> by his or her peers, this behavior lessens the child's
        9

feelings of love and acceptance, which are necessary for success in school.

Only when food, sleep, love, safety, and confidence <u>are existed</u> in a child's
                                                        10

life will the child be able to express creativity and curiosity at school. As much

as schools try to overcome the obstacles in a child's life, the child's future

<u>will be influence</u> directly by the home environment.
    11

4. *The following paragraph has ten errors in the use of the passive voice. Find and correct the errors.*

It is widely believe that the attack on Pearl Harbor caused American

intolerance toward the Japanese, but anti-Japanese sentiments can be tracing

back much earlier to the time when the first Japanese immigrants began

to enter the United States in hopes of finding a better life. The Japanese

immigrants were become expert farmers and competed against Americans

for land rights and farm business. The Japanese soon were seeing as such a

problem that a law was passing to allow only the Japanese who had already

owned homes in the United States to enter the country. The Japanese were

eventually label as heathens, and it was assume that they were unable to

assimilate into American culture. Like immigrants of earlier times, the

Japanese worked longer hours and for lower wages than citizens who were born in America. After the laundry business had been entering by the Japanese, white workers organized the "Anti-Jap Laundry League." During election years, racist attacks against the Japanese multiplied. In fact, in 1906 the San Francisco school board had laws pass to segregate Japanese American students within the school district. Although the bombing of Pearl Harbor did not improve the reputation of the Japanese in the United States, it is clear that years earlier anti-Japanese sentiment had accepted as a part of life.

WRITING TOPICS

Most academic essays and research papers require an introduction with a strong thesis statement. The paragraphs following the introduction support the thesis with references to outside sources. These outside sources might be summarized, quoted, or paraphrased. Notice how the following body paragraph, which was taken from a longer piece of writing, includes a topic sentence, a body with support from outside sources, and a concluding sentence. Use this paragraph as a model when you write about one of the following topics.

Study the use of the active and passive voice in the following student paragraph. Circle the six verbs that are in the passive voice and two participial adjectives.

Amelia Earhart is one of the most famous aviators in American history. Although she set numerous flying records and wrote many books, she is best known for being the first female aviator to fly solo across the Atlantic Ocean. In 1937 while Earhart was attempting to fly around the world, her plane crashed in the Pacific Ocean, and she was never seen again. Because of her many successes, a statue of Amelia Earhart has been commissioned for Statuary Hall in the U.S. Capitol. The statue of Earhart will be funded by Equal Visibility Everywhere (EVE), a women's organization. In *Ms. Magazine*, Lynette Long, president of EVE, stated that "Amelia Earhart was one of the most inspiring women in American history . . . She's still a role model for girls everywhere, and the prospect of having her in Statuary Hall is incredibly exciting."[1] The Earhart statue will be one of ten statues of women that are featured in the U.S. Capitol. For all Americans but for girls in particular, the statue of Amelia Earhart in one of the most important buildings in the country will be a message that anything can be achieved if one believes that it is important.

[1] "Amelia Earhart Statue to Be Added to Capitol," *Ms. Magazine*, September 2, 2010, http://www.msmagazine.com/news/uswirestory.asp?ID=12613.

Choose one of the topics below and write at least one paragraph. Find an outside source to support the ideas that you present in your writing. Use the passive voice and participial adjectives. After you complete your first draft, concentrate on editing your work. Keep in mind the editing practice from this chapter.

1. Should the arts be included in the curriculum for elementary and high school students? Why or why not? Think about how our later lives are influenced by the arts and whether training children in them is a good investment.

2. Select an important structure such as a building or statue. Discuss the structure's history. Why was it built? Who constructed it? When was it created? Why is it important to you or to society?

Go to page 167 for more practice with the passive voice.

Modals

GRAMMAR FOCUS

Modals function much like other verbs; they have several forms and occur in different time frames. Therefore, like verb tenses, it is important to study and practice using the different forms and functions of modals. Notice the role that the modals in the following sentences play in the meaning and form of each sentence.

SIMPLE PRESENT/NECESSITY	The government **must make** Internet access a priority in all locations of the country.
FUTURE PROGRESSIVE/POSSIBILITY	The Congress **may be passing** legislation soon to fund Internet access in remote locations of the country.
SIMPLE PAST (PASSIVE)/SUGGESTION	Internet providers **should have been given** government funding years ago to develop Internet access in remote locations.

Pretest

Check your understanding of modals. Put a check (✓) next to the sentences that are correct.

_____ **1.** Because the body stores carbohydrates, a low-carb diet may being effective in weight loss.

_____ **2.** Many paleontologists believe that an asteroid might have killed the dinosaurs while others believe it was the spread of disease.

_____ **3.** Although not everyone agrees, many argue that mobile phones should be banning from all public places.

_____ **4.** The Hubble Space Telescope should be explore the solar system for at least the next few years.

_____ **5.** Some biologists believe that because ice was found on the moon, humans will be able to live there with the right technology.

_____ **6.** Americans must not have been exercising regularly over the past decades as the obesity rate has continually been increasing.

_____ **7.** A 20/20 vision standard must be meeting to be a pilot of any military aircraft.

_____ **8.** Some environmentalists discourage the use of Styrofoam, which they believe should have harmed land, water, and air quality.

_____ **9.** Using plastic rather than wood would have saved money in the building of the theater's scenery.

_____ **10.** Athletes had better to train often to compete successfully.

Notice how the following paragraph uses five different modals. Circle each modal as you read the paragraph. Use what you already know about modals to write down each modal's tense and purpose: ability, possibility, necessity, suggestion, or expectation.

On average between 500,000 and 600,000 people are homeless every day in the United States. Logic tells us that as economic prosperity increases, homelessness should decrease. However, this is not the case. People who study homelessness think this may be because housing costs are expensive, wages are low, and urban areas remain depressed. To decrease the number of homeless on the street, government and citizens must work together to locate housing for this segment of our population. In addition, the homeless ought to have access to medical care and job opportunities. When society focuses on a problem like homelessness, it can solve the problem and make life better for both the homeless and the housed.

FORMING MODALS

1. Modals in the present time frame have two main forms.

Modal + base verb
Newborn infants **can focus** *on objects 7 to 12 inches away from their eyes.*

Modal + *be* + present participle
Later, babies **may be observing** *objects in the distance but responding only to those within 7 to 12 inches.*

- Phrasal modals in the present use the regular present forms.

be able to
Newborn infants **are able to digest** *milk immediately after birth.*

have to
An infant **has to cry** *in order to express hunger, fear, and other emotions.*

be supposed to
Infants **are supposed to form** *attachments early for proper emotional development later in life.*

2. Modals in the past time frame have two main forms.

Modal + *have* + past participle
The eruption of Krakatoa volcano in 1883 **may have killed** *over 40,000 people.*

Modal + *have* + *been* + present participle
Islanders near Krakatoa **should have been preparing** *for the eruption because of numerous smaller eruptions during the preceding months.*

- Phrasal modals in the past use the regular past forms.

be able to
People **were able to hear** *the eruption of Krakatoa 3,000 miles away.*

have to
After Krakatoa's eruption in 1883, survivors **had to run** *to high ground to avoid the resulting tsunami.*

be supposed to
Additional volcanic islands **were supposed to form** *after the eruption of Krakatoa.*

3. Modals in the future time frame have the same forms as modals in the present time frame. Time expressions are usually used to make the future time clear.

> Modal + base verb
> *Rising ocean temperatures **may kill** the ocean's coral reefs within the next few decades.*

> Modal + *be* + present participle
> *International organizations **should be establishing** laws that protect the world's reefs in the coming years.*

- Phrasal modals in the future use *will* or *be going to*.

be able to	*Some countries **will be able to build** artificial reefs to replace the dead reefs.*
have to	*Humans **are going to have to** slow rising ocean temperatures to save the world's reefs.*
be supposed to	No future form

WRITING TIP

In formal academic writing, it is best not to use contractions. However, when contractions with modals are appropriate in your writing, follow these rules. In their negative forms, the modals *can, could, would,* and *should* use the contractions *can't, couldn't, wouldn't,* and *shouldn't.* Do not use the negative contraction for the modals *may, might,* and *must.* For these modals, use the uncontracted forms *may not, might not,* and *must not.*

---

4. Some modals are irregular and do not use the usual forms in the present, past, and future.

- *Had better* is a phrasal modal in the present.

  *Nonprofit organizations **had better use** most of their funds for appropriate purposes or people will stop donating.*

The past form of *had better* is *had better have* + past participle.

> *Regions with bad hurricanes **had better have developed** disaster plans to lessen the problems of future hurricanes.*

NOTE: In informal writing and spoken English, *had better* can form a contraction with a pronoun.

I'd/You'd/He'd/She'd/It'd/We'd/They'd better learn *cardiopulmonary resuscitation (CPR) before working in a hospital.*

- When showing ability, the past form of the modal *can* is *could.*

  *Various scientific methods can detect volcanic activity today, but in 1883 they **could not predict** Krakatoa's eruption.*

5. Modals can also be used in the passive voice in the present and past.

> Present   Modal + *be* + past participle
> *Space tourism **must be regulated** by governmental agencies.*

> Past   Modal + *have* + *been* + past participle
> *Some people believe that private space travel **should have been stopped** before it began.*

WRITING TIP

Check that you are using the correct past participle form by checking its form in a dictionary or Appendix 2 at the back of this book.

Circle the sentence that forms the modal correctly.

1. **(a)** English students must to submit their papers to a plagiarism detection Web site.

   (b) English students must submit their papers to a plagiarism detection Web site.

2. **(a)** Newspapers and magazines may not survive in their current forms.

   (b) Newspapers and magazines mayn't survive in their current forms.

3. **(a)** Some say that the pioneers of the future may be to live in outer space, colonizing habitable planets.

   (b) Some say that the pioneers of the future may be living in outer space, colonizing habitable planets.

4. **(a)** Diseases such as schizophrenia are believed to be genetic; however, they could also been caused by traumatic events.

   (b) Diseases such as schizophrenia are believed to be genetic; however, they could also be caused by traumatic events.

5. **(a)** Telephone companies had better have already developed a plan to compete with Internet phone providers or they will soon be losing customers.

   (b) Telephone companies had better have already to develop a plan to compete with Internet phone providers or they will soon be losing customers.

USING MODALS

MEANING	PRESENT AND FUTURE	PAST
To show ability **can** **be able to**	Today computers **can process** information at approximately 3 GHz. Modern computer monitors **are able to display** all colors. Computer engineers **will be able to improve** monitor color and clarity in future computer generations.	The first computers **could process** information at a rate of 2 MHz. Original computer monitors **were able to show** only amber and green colors.
To show possibility **can** **may** **might** **could**	Mediation **can be** an alternative to standard legal processes in resolving conflicts. Mediation **may be** an effective way to resolve 90 percent of all disputes. Mediation **might be** a solution to the overcrowded court system. Mediators **could play** an important role in law firms.	No past form Some divorced couples **may have found** effective solutions to their disagreements through mediation. Mediation **might have been** better than prosecution for some drug cases in the past. Mediators **could have resolved** many important disputes in past decades.

MEANING	PRESENT AND FUTURE	PAST
To show near certainty (deduction) **must** **would**	Because of the presence of water, there **must be** life on other planets. Life **would be** possible in outer space under the right conditions.	Evidence tells us that life **must have existed** on other planets in the past. Life **would have existed** on planets where evidence of water exists.
To show necessity **must** **have to/have got to**	Medical doctors **must complete** a minimum of four years of medical school and three to seven years of residency training. Medical school students **have to devote** their first two years to book study and laboratory work. Medical students **will have to study** various alternative forms of medicine in the future.	No past form In the Islamic world, doctors **had to attend** medical school as far back as 872.
To show lack of necessity **do not + have to**	Medical doctors **do not have to study** alternative forms of medicine such as acupuncture, homeopathy, and hypnosis. Within a few years, doctors **will not have to work** with health insurance companies as much as they do today.	In the mid-1800s in the United States, doctors **did not have to attend** medical school to practice medicine.
To show prohibition **must not** **cannot**	Physicians **must not assist** in ending a person's life. Physicians **cannot charge** fees that are above what is considered reasonable for the procedure.	No past form No past form
To give advice/make suggestions **had better (not)** **should** **ought to** **could** **can**	The police **had better control** gang violence. Community organizations **should help** the police in controlling gang membership. Law enforcement **ought to know** why youths want to join gangs. Law enforcement **could place** undercover officers in the gangs. Schools and families **can assist** law enforcement with decreasing gang membership.	The police **had better have controlled** the gang violence on the streets last night. Community organizations **should have helped** the police in controlling gang membership in the past. Law enforcement **ought to have known** why youths wanted to join gangs years ago. Law enforcement **could have placed** undercover officers in the gangs last year. No past form
To show expectation **be supposed to** **should** **ought to**	Divorce rates **are supposed to decrease** as fewer people marry in the future. The number of marriages **should increase** next year as tax advantages improve for married couples. The number of unwed mothers **ought to continue** rising as society accepts this social trend in coming years.	Divorce rates **were supposed to decrease,** but they increased instead. Births by unwed mothers **should have risen,** but they declined instead. The trend toward marriage at an older age **ought to have improved** the divorce rate in the past decade.

MEANING	PRESENT AND FUTURE	PAST
To make requests can could would	**Can** you read my paper and give me advice on it? **Could** you take my homework to class for me? **Would** you help me edit my paper?	No past form No past form No past form
To show preference would rather	Most law students report that they **would rather work** for a large firm than a small firm.	Many paralegals **would rather have become** lawyers, but they didn't because of the time or money necessary to pursue a law degree.
To show a repeated action would	No present or future form	In the past, when Chinese students wanted to study in the United States, they **would have** trouble getting student visas.

NOTE: Another use of *would* is as the past tense of *will*.

> *Many people hope that scientists **will discover** the cure for cancer within the coming decade.*

> *At a medical conference last year, many scientists learned that researchers **would** soon **find** the cure for most forms of cancer.*

WRITING TIP

A phrasal modal is generally more informal than its corresponding one-word modal.

Formal: *People **must recycle** their waste to improve the environment.*

Less formal: *People **have to recycle** their waste to improve the environment.*

The opposite is true for *can* and *be able to.*

Formal: *Cities **are able to improve** their environment by recycling.*

Less formal: *Cities **can improve** their environment by recycling.*

---

1. The simple and progressive modal forms occur in slightly different circumstances. Just like the simple present, modal + base verb implies that something is a fact or always true, while the progressive forms, modal + *be* + present participle, refer to an action that is/was happening at a specific moment in the present or the past.

> *Apple trees **should bear** fruit in the fall.* (This is a fact that is always true.)

> *The apple orchards in the Northwest **should be producing** fruit right now.* (This is an action that is happening right now for a limited period of time.)

> *Orchard workers **should have been harvesting** the apple crop last month.* (This is an action that was happening for a limited period of time in the past.)

> *Improved public transportation **could eliminate** some air pollution.* (This is a fact that is always true.)

> *Currently ethanol buses **could be helping** in the reduction of carbon emissions.* (This is an action that is happening right now and may be happening for only a limited period of time.)

> *Energy plants **could have been producing** energy from alternative forms years ago.* (This is an action that had a possibility of happening over a period of time in the past but did not.)

WRITING TIP

In spoken English, the modals *must* and *can/could* are frequently used to show disbelief in the present and past.

The professor **must be joking**! *We* **can't be having** *an exam today!*

The professor **must have been kidding**! *He* **couldn't have expected** *us to know all the formulas by yesterday!*

This informal use of *must* and *can/could* is rarely used in written English.

2. Using modals in the passive voice occurs under the same circumstances as all other verbs that use the passive voice. Use modals in the passive voice in the following circumstances:

- when the person or thing doing the action (the agent) is obvious, unknown, or unimportant.

    Present: *The public* **should be informed** *of its community's crime rates.*

    Past: *Urban murder rates* **ought to have been reduced**.

- when you don't want to mention the person doing the action or you want to be discrete.

    Present: *Racial profiling* **could be used** *to deport certain groups of people.*

    Past: *Crime rates* **may have been altered** *to make the city appear safe.*

- when you want to emphasize the receiver of the action or the result of the action.

    Present: *Crime victims* **must be treated** *with the utmost respect.*

    Past: *In the past, crime victims* **may have been regarded** *as a problem rather than as part of the solution to a crime.*

- when you are describing a process.

    Present: *Now the evidence* **can be taken** *to the crime lab where it* **must be examined** *and* **placed** *into the crime report.*

    Past: *The evidence* **was supposed to be collected** *a few hours ago.*

- when you want your writing to sound objective.

    Present: *It* **may be found** *that the crime evidence was fabricated.*

    Past: *It* **should have been discovered** *earlier that the crime evidence was fabricated.*

- when you introduce new information in the first sentence with the active voice and expand on that information in the following sentence with the passive voice.

    Present: *Law enforcement has been experimenting with new methods to reduce crime rates. These methods* **may be applied** *in the coming years in crime-ridden environments.*

    Past: *Law enforcement was developing new crime reduction methods. These methods* **should have been used** *to reduce crime in urban areas.*

3. *Would, could,* and *should* + *have* + past participle usually refer to an action that was started but was not completed or was not successful. These modals express probability based on evidence; they do not express definite facts.

> *The economy* **would have recovered** *by now.* (if something had happened, but it didn't)

> *The Congress* **could have passed** *laws to stimulate the economy.* (but it chose not to do this)

> *The president* **should have pushed** *harder for economic reform.* (however, he did not do this)

NOTE: These forms are commonly used in conditional sentences with if clauses. Refer to Chapter 6 in this book for more practice with these modal forms.

4. Both *can* and *could* are often used in the simple present to show possibility, but *can* shows a more definite possibility than *could.*

Strong possibility:	*Tuberculosis* **can spread** *from person to person through the air.*
Weak possibility:	*Some believe that tuberculosis* **could** *also* **spread** *by contact with infected dirt.*

5. Use *would, used to,* and *be used to* + present participle to write about habits or actions that happen repeatedly.

Past habit or repeated action:	*Colonizers* **would imprison** *and sometimes* **massacre** *indigenous people.*
	Colonizers **used to isolate** *native cultures on reservations.*
	Indigenous people **were used to having** *total freedom before colonization.*
Present habit:	*Indigenous people* **are used to fighting** *for their rights.*

Self Check 2

Circle the sentence that uses the modal correctly.

1. (a) Andrea should wait at the airport when you arrive.

  (b) Andrea should be waiting at the airport when you arrive.

2. (a) The gold nugget might sell for a million dollars at auction.

  (b) The gold nugget does not have to sell for a million dollars at auction.

3. (a) In the United States, polio used to be common during the summer months.

  (b) In the United States, polio was used to being common during the summer months.

4. (a) The curators at the natural history museum completed the dinosaur display, but their budget was cut and all work stopped.

  (b) The curators at the natural history museum would have completed the dinosaur display, but their budget was cut and all work stopped.

5. (a) Lack of proper ventilation in laboratories could be caused dangerous side effects when scientists are working with toxic fumes.

(b) Lack of proper ventilation in laboratories could cause dangerous side effects when scientists are working with toxic fumes.

EDITING PRACTICE

1. *Put a check (✓) next to the sentences that form and use modals correctly. Correct the sentences that have errors. There may be more than one way to correct some errors.*

_____ **1.** Articles in the student newspaper are supposed to be written from the perspective of the students.

_____ **2.** When teachers are not in class, they have to be grading papers.

_____ **3.** Inferior electrical work may have cause the fire that burned down the warehouse.

_____ **4.** To ensure their own health and the health of their patients, doctors can follow safety procedures during surgery.

_____ **5.** Everyday household products such as disinfectants, air fresheners, and cleaners would be dangerous to human health.

_____ **6.** New animals at the zoo must to be kept in quarantine before they are moved to their permanent locations.

_____ **7.** All scientific hypotheses ought to be thoroughly tested for accuracy before they are considered factual.

_____ **8.** Israeli Prime Minister Yitzhak Rabin would have signed a peace accord, but he was assassinated in 1995.

_____ **9.** Hawaiians had better preserve their language or it will soon become extinct.

_____ **10.** Amtrak will be supposed to complete the new rapid rail system next year.

_____ **11.** College students who place too much personal information on social networking sites must have problems getting jobs after graduation.

_____ **12.** One employee with low morale could erode the attitude of all other employees in the office.

2. *Read the following paragraph. Complete the paragraph by circling the correct modal phrase.*

Scholars believe that written forms of poetry

_____ at the dawn of civilization. Collections
        1. had better have existed / may have existed

of poetry from the ancient civilizations of Mesopotamia and Egypt exist in

several books that _____ from the time
                        2. can be dated / could be dated

when those two regions prospered. It _____
                                    3. can be argued / can argue

that the written form of poetry _____ first
                                4. might have emerged / might be emerging

in one of those two areas, for it is there that the most ancient form of written

language, pictographs, existed. Although it is believed that writing first began

in the southern region of Mesopotamia known as Sumer, recent evidence of

Egyptian writing that _____ this has been
                        5. may predate / may be predated

found. According to an article in *The New York Times* by author John Noble

Wilford, a 5,250-year-old tableau was discovered by archaeologists who

argue it _____ the world's earliest historical
            6. may have been / may be

document. This _____ important evidence
                7. would be / would being

that the first true writing _____ in Egypt
                            8. might have originated / might originate

and not in ancient Sumer as scholars had believed. These findings remain

controversial; nevertheless, it still _____ that
                                    9. would be assumed / can be assumed

written poetry first emerged during ancient times in this region of the world.

3. *In the following paragraph, the underlined modals are not correct. Write the correct tense or form of the modal above each underlined error. There may be more than one way to correct some errors.*

One interesting outcome of the Industrial Revolution was the advent

of the department store. As machines started to replace workers in factories,

products <u>could be producing</u> at high rates of speed. These mass-produced

1

goods led to the birth of department stores, where all these goods <u>could found</u>

                                                                               2

in one location at affordable prices. The first department stores <u>may be created</u>

                                                                                    3

what historian William Leach called the "Land of Desire." These stores

<u>must carry</u> everything the consumers wished for, and their advertisements

4

<u>could be making</u> consumers believe that they needed these products. When

5

the customers <u>would walked</u> into a department store, they would no longer

                       6

feel like middle- or working-class citizens—they <u>must feel</u> as though they were

                                                              7

from a higher class: being taken care of by employees

who <u>would responded</u> to all their needs and walking

    8

through buildings full of the latest fashions

and technological advances of the time, including

escalators, electric lighting, and cash registers. Like

department stores today, the first department stores

<u>use to spend</u> millions on advertisements to draw in

9

customers to buy their products. Although many of

the advances of the Industrial Revolution were

surpassed in the following years, the department store

<u>may have been</u> one of the few legacies of the

10

Industrial Revolution that hasn't changed

significantly.

4. *The following paragraphs have ten errors in the form and use of modals. Find and correct the errors. There may be more than one way to correct some errors.*

Although many people today should not have heard of Clarence Earl Gideon, he changed the American legal system in a very important way. Gideon was accused of a robbery in Florida in 1961. At his trial, he requested a lawyer because he couldn't have afforded his own, but the judge denied Gideon's request. In the end, Gideon, who could not defending himself as well as a trained lawyer, lost his case and was sentenced to five years in the state penitentiary. In jail, he was able to studied constitutional law and discovered that he might of been denied his Sixth Amendment right that says defendants who are not able afford their own attorneys must be providing one by the state. Without a lawyer to defend Gideon, his trial had not been fair. Gideon appealed to the Supreme Court and was granted a retrial. In the second trial, thanks to his court-appointed lawyer, Gideon was found not guilty. Many prisoners took an interest in Gideon's case, for many were tried without lawyers and will be eligible for retrial just like Gideon.

After these proceedings, the "Gideon Rule" was established. It upheld the Sixth Amendment's promise of counsel to all people regardless of race, age, or financial situation. Immediately following Gideon's case, several more "Gideons," poor and uneducated defendants who cannot provide a lawyer for their defense, were able to been saved with the help of court-appointed counsel.

WRITING TOPICS

Most academic essays and research papers require an introduction with a strong thesis statement. The body paragraphs following the introduction support the thesis with references to outside sources. These outside sources might be summarized, quoted, or paraphrased. Notice how the following body paragraph, which was taken from a longer piece of writing, includes a topic sentence, a body with support from outside sources, and a concluding sentence. Use this paragraph as a model when you write about one of the following topics.

Study the use of modals in the following student paragraph. Put a check on the lines where the eight modals appear. Decide the purpose of each modal: ability, possibility, necessity, etc.

Before European settlement, Australia was inhabited by Aboriginal people and Torres Straight Islanders. When large numbers of Europeans settled Australia in the 1700s and 1800s, many indigenous people became ill and died, while the others were not able to maintain their traditional lifestyle. During this period, Australia was becoming a wealthy country because of its farming, mining, and trade. In 1901, the Commonwealth of Australia was established with about 100,000 indigenous people and 4 million others primarily from England, Scotland, and Ireland. Australians must have wanted to maintain their English roots because they passed the Immigration Restriction Act that limited immigration to Europeans only. As presented in "Australia in Brief: Ancient Heritage, Modern Society," most Australians today feel this law should not have passed; immigrants from over 200 countries currently live in Australia.[1] In addition to Australia's strength in farming, mining, and trade, tourism should be added. Because of the approximately 6 million tourists who travel to Australia each year, tourism may soon be Australia's biggest business. Sports are another important part of the Australian lifestyle. In order to be considered truly Australian, one has to compete in several sports. This belief might have begun as a result of the beautiful weather and outdoor lifestyle that is possible in Australia. Because of Australia's location as one of the Pacific Rim countries, its future should be bright as its neighboring countries become wealthier and more important in world politics.

---

[1] "Australia in Brief: Ancient Heritage, Modern Society," Australian Government Department of Foreign Affairs and Trade, accessed July 14, 2011, http://www.dfat.gov.au/aib/history.html.

Choose one of the topics below and write at least one paragraph. Find an outside source to support the ideas that you present in your writing. Use a variety of modals in different forms and tenses. After you complete your first draft, concentrate on editing your work. Keep in mind the editing practice from this chapter.

1. Compare and/or contrast what school life was like in your country when you were studying there and what school life is like in the country where you now live. When you describe school life in your country, think about what you used to do or would do, what you could have or should have done, and what you had to do. Then describe these same actions or situations in the country where you now live. Finally, discuss the results of the differences between the two countries in terms of graduation rates, who enters university and who doesn't, how the school system affects the country's economy and people's job prospects, and so on.

2. Select one country in the world to research briefly. Choose a country that you are unfamiliar with. What industry is the most profitable in this country? What industry is growing the fastest? What are the high school and university graduation rates? What is the government like? How does or doesn't this country preserve its natural resources? Use this information to make some deductions or educated guesses about what is and isn't important to the people of this country. Use your research to explain what might be possible or impossible for this country in the future.

Go to page 169 for more practice with modals.

Nouns and Determiners

GRAMMAR FOCUS

The prevalence of nouns and determiners in all types of writing makes it necessary to practice applying the complicated rules that govern their use. Study how the following two sentences use the same noun, *television*, but in one instance it is an uncountable noun and in the other it is countable. This difference changes the meaning of the noun, affects the choice of determiner, and influences the subject-verb agreement.

> **Television provides** valuable information to most of the world today.

> **One or two televisions are** part of most households in industrialized countries.

This chapter will allow you to review and practice using these important differences involving nouns and determiners.

Pretest

Check your understanding of nouns and determiners. Put a check (✓) next to the sentences that are correct.

_____ **1.** The best way to learn a new language is through the immersion.

_____ **2.** The city of Syracuse suspended use of heating oil for five day to meet its energy goal.

_____ **3.** Taxes placed on imports angered early settlers of country.

_____ **4.** The president of the United States met with the president of China to discuss ways to strengthen their diplomatic ties.

_____ **5.** Mitochondrial RNA is passed on only from that mother.

_____ **6.** Air turbulences occur when airplanes fly over rough patches of air.

_____ **7.** Statistical data are easily manipulated to support false claims.

_____ **8.** By no longer giving out peanuts on every flights, airlines have been able to save millions of dollars.

_____ **9.** Visual learners are usually good spellers.

_____ **10.** One of the most common causes of death worldwide is the diarrhea.

The following paragraph uses different types of nouns and determiners. Several determiners are circled. Draw an arrow from the circled determiner to its noun. Notice if the noun is plural or singular, countable or uncountable.

On Sunday morning, December 7, 1941, (the) residents of Pearl Harbor woke up to the sound of fighter planes attacking from (the) sky. As the bombs found (their) targets on the naval base, American battleships and airstrips were destroyed. The Japanese had successfully launched (a) surprise attack on Pearl Harbor. At the time, (this) attack was the most violent act of a foreign nation on American soil, killing over (2,400) Americans. After the attack, it was obvious that (much) more intelligence was needed to avoid (another) similar attack on the mainland of the United States. By December 8, 1941, (every) American was anxious to help with the war effort and inspired by the slogan "Remember December 7th!"

NOUNS

1. There are several different types of nouns. Count nouns, nouns that we are able to count, are the most common in English.

   - Most count nouns use the plural –s, –es, or –ies ending or in some cases have irregular plural forms.

church — churches	knife — knives
city — cities	man — men
crisis — crises	mouse — mice
foot — feet	pencil — pencils

   NOTE: Refer to a dictionary if you are uncertain about how to spell the plural form.

   - Some count nouns use the same form for singular and plural. These are typically names of animals.

bison	salmon
deer	sheep
moose	swine

   - Some academic count nouns come from Greek or Latin and do not follow the usual rules for forming plurals.

alumnus — alumni	hypothesis — hypotheses
analysis — analyses	index — indices
axis — axes	nucleus — nuclei
criterion — criteria	phenomenon — phenomena
datum — data	vertebra — vertebrae
fungus — fungi	

   - Some count nouns are most commonly used in their plural forms.

agenda	criteria
bacteria	data

WRITING TIP

Proper nouns and proper adjectives are always capitalized.

One of the fastest growing religions is **Catholicism**. (proper noun)

In many countries, **Catholic** schools educate the majority of children. (proper adjective)

---

2. Uncountable nouns, nouns that we cannot count, do not have plural forms because they do not represent distinct objects. These nouns use the third-person singular verb.

   Research takes a lot of time to do well.

   Hunger was the main topic of discussion at the meeting of the United Nations World Food Programme.

There are several different types of uncountable nouns. They include:

Whole groups made up of individual parts: *equipment, furniture, homework, information, money, traffic,* etc.

Abstract nouns (general concepts or ideas): *anger, advice, cooperation, courage, curiosity, democracy, fear, freedom, happiness, health, honesty, hunger, knowledge, laziness, patience, poverty, research, wealth, wisdom,* etc.

Solid materials and substances, including food: *bread, butter, gold, iron, jam, lettuce, meat, metal, paper, silver, wood, yogurt,* etc.

Liquid materials and substances: *blood, coffee, juice, milk, oil, tea, water,* etc.

Grains or particles: *dirt, dust, pepper, rice, sand, salt, sugar,* etc.

Natural occurrences, including weather: *electricity, fire, fog, heat, ice, light, pollution, rain, snow, wind,* etc.

Gases: *air, oxygen, smoke, smog, steam,* etc.

Fields of study: *art, chemistry, history, mathematics, music, physics,* etc.

Languages: *Arabic, Chinese, English, French, Greek, Russian, Spanish,* etc.

Physical conditions: *arthritis, cancer, influenza, measles, pneumonia,* etc.

3. Some uncountable nouns end with an *–s* but are still not countable and use the third-person singular verb.

acoustics	linguistics	physics	species
ethics	mechanics	series	

Linguistics is *the science of language and* **includes** *phonetics, phonology, syntax, and semantics.*

4. Collective nouns are nouns that describe groups that have members.

- Collective nouns are generally singular because the members work together to accomplish a common goal; therefore, they use the third-person singular verb. However, collective nouns may be plural and use the plural verb form when the members work as individuals, not as a group.

army	class	faculty	group	majority/minority
audience	committee	family	jury	team

The **faculty meets** *in* **its** *conference room every Friday for lunch.*

Some **faculty disagree** *with* **their** *dean's decisions.*

The **family works** *together to take care of* **its** *youngest and oldest members.*

My **family have** *disagreed about how to take care of* **their** *oldest family members.*

- Some collective nouns use the plural verb form. Most of these collective nouns come from adjectives that describe people.

military
police
the blind/deaf/disabled/elderly/homeless/poor/rich/unemployed/young

> The **elderly face** many challenges in the workforce. **They** may find it difficult to find a job.
>
> The **disabled were** discriminated against in the past. Today, **they** are treated as equal members of society.

5. Some nouns have a singular meaning but have only a plural form and use a plural verb.

binoculars	jeans	pliers
clothes	pajamas	scissors
glasses	pants	shorts

> **Jeans have been** the most popular form of clothing since the 1960s. **They** have not been replaced by any other style of pants.

6. Some nouns are both countable and uncountable, depending on whether the writer is referring to the noun in general (uncountable meaning) or a specific kind or instance (count meaning). Use a determiner to show a specific instance of the noun (the "countable noun.")

aspirin	chicken	crime	juice	pastry	turkey
beauty	chocolate	education	law	tea	water
cheese	coffee	glass	life	truth	wine

> **Education** is an important political issue in most elections. (general meaning)
>
> All people should have access to **a good education**. (specific meaning)
>
> **Aspirin** helps to relieve pain. (general meaning)
>
> Many people with heart disease take **an aspirin** every day. (specific meaning)

WRITING TIP

Check a dictionary if you are unsure of the plural form of a noun or are using the noun for the first time.

Self Check 1

Circle the sentence that uses nouns correctly.

1. (a) Naguib Mahfouz said you can judge a man's wisdoms by the questions he asks.

  (b) Naguib Mahfouz said you can judge a man's wisdom by the questions he asks.

2. **(a)** Many wildlife programs have been formed to protect endangered species like the Chinese panda.

   (b) Many wildlife programs have been formed to protect an endangered specie like the Chinese panda.

3. **(a)** The unemployed was first helped by unemployment insurance in Wisconsin in 1932.

   (b) The unemployed were first helped by unemployment insurance in Wisconsin in 1932.

4. **(a)** The biggest issue in the last election was prevention of crime.

   (b) The biggest issue in the last election was prevention of a crime.

5. **(a)** Tobacco and cotton were the basis of the southern economy for decades.

   (b) Tobacco and cotton were the basises of the southern economy for decades.

DETERMINERS

Determiners include the following different types. Review how each type of determiner is used with the nouns in the chart below.

Articles

   Indefinite: *a, an*

   Definite: *the*

Quantifiers: *another, a few, each, some, much,* etc.

Demonstrative adjectives: *this, that, these, those*

Possessives

   Adjectives: *my, your, his, her, its, one's, our, their*

   Nouns: *Jenny's, my professor's, two students',* etc.

Numbers: *one, two, tenth, twentieth,* etc.

	SINGULAR	PLURAL
Count nouns • indefinite article / no article • definite article • quantifier • demonstrative adjective • possessive adjective • possessive noun • number	a pencil the pencil each pencil this pencil his pencil a student's pencil one pencil	pencils the pencils a few pencils these pencils my pencils Lupita's pencils six pencils
Uncountable nouns • no determiner • definite article • quantifier • demonstrative adjective • possessive adjective • possessive noun	luggage the luggage a little luggage this/that luggage her luggage the team's luggage	

ARTICLES

When deciding which article to use, you need to know whether a noun is a count noun or an uncountable noun. This diagram will help you decide which articles can be used with which nouns.

Summary of Article Usage

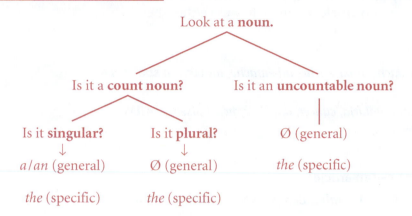

1. Use the indefinite article *a* or *an* with singular count nouns to introduce a topic for the first time or to indicate a general meaning.

    A *computer with additional memory will perform quickly.*

    An *alternative energy source may soon replace fossil fuel.*

WRITING TIP

Use *a* with nouns and adjectives that begin with a consonant sound and *an* with nouns and adjectives that begin with a vowel sound.

*There is not **a common currency** for the countries in Asia; however, there is **a European** currency for most countries within the European Union.*

*When traveling, it is essential to allow **an adequate amount** of time for security checks. Airport officials recommend that travelers arrive at least **an hour** before their departure.*

---

2. Use the definite article *the* with singular or plural count nouns and with uncountable nouns when the reader and writer know which noun is being discussed or when the noun is specific within a setting. Use the following list to help determine when to use the definite article:

    • the noun is specific for all people: *the sun, the moon, the earth*

    • the noun is specific within a location: *the living room, the counter, the floor*

    • the noun is specific for a group of people: *the Prime Minister, the textbook, the meeting*

    • the noun is specific because of unique characteristics: *the crash, the earthquake, the riot*

    • the noun is specific because it has already been mentioned: *There was an earthquake in Chile. The earthquake registered 7.1 on the Richter Scale.*

    • the noun is specific because of its rank within a group: *the first, the fastest, the best*

    • the noun is specific because of a defining adjective, phrase, or clause: *the Dell computer, the book on the desk, the paper that is due tomorrow*

3. Use no article with plural count nouns and uncountable nouns to make a generalization about a total group of things, objects, or concepts.

> **Cars** *can be expensive and inconvenient in many large cities.* (all cars in general)

> **Public transportation** *is inexpensive and quick in many large cities.* (public transportation in general)

4. The names of some sicknesses use the definite article, and others use the indefinite article, whereas some use no article (ø) and a few use either the definite article or ø.

> definite article: *the flu, the plague*

> indefinite article: *a cold, a headache, a backache, an earache, an ulcer, a stroke, a heart attack*

> no article: *influenza, pneumonia, malaria, cancer, diarrhea, heart disease, AIDS, herpes, diabetes, rabies*

> no article or *the*: *chickenpox, measles, hiccups*

5. Most geographical names do not use an article.

> Continents: *Africa, Antarctica, Asia, Australia, Europe, North America, South America*

> Countries: *Brazil, China, Iceland, Korea, Germany, Mexico,* etc.

> Cities: *Los Angeles, Melbourne, Seoul, Tehran, Tokyo,* etc.

> Lakes and seas: *Aral Sea, Caspian Sea, Lake Superior, Lake Victoria,* etc.

> Islands: *Fiji, Hokkaido, Maui, Santorini,* etc.

> Bays: *Bay of Bengal, Bay of Islands, San Francisco Bay,* etc.

> Parks: *Central Park, Yellowstone National Park, Stanley Park,* etc.

> Streets, roads, and avenues: *Lexington Avenue, Main Street, 10th Boulevard,* etc.

Some geographical names use the definite article because the name refers to a group composed of smaller parts. Some, like the names of oceans, simply use the definite article and their names must be memorized.

> Countries: *the Soviet Union, the United Kingdom, the United States,* etc.

> Islands: *the Caribbean Islands, the Marshall Islands, the Philippines,* etc.

> Lakes: *the Great Lakes,* etc.

> Mountain ranges: *the Alps, the Caucasus, the Rockies,* etc.

> Oceans: *the Atlantic Ocean, the Arctic Ocean, the Indian Ocean, the Pacific Ocean*

QUANTIFIERS AND NUMBERS

Quantifiers and numbers allow writers to show an amount for the noun that follows the quantifier or number. There are many quantifiers and rules for using them. Study the types of nouns that pair with some of the most common quantifiers in the following chart.

COUNT NOUNS (SINGULAR)	COUNT NOUNS (PLURAL)	UNCOUNTABLE NOUNS	PLURAL COUNTABLE AND UNCOUNTABLE NOUNS
each student every student another student one student	each of the students many students (not) many students many of the students a few students (very) few students several students a great number of students a great many students a couple of/both students ten students	much traffic (not) much traffic too much traffic a little traffic (very) little traffic a great deal of traffic a large amount of traffic less traffic none of the traffic	some students/traffic a lot of students/traffic lots of students/traffic plenty of students/traffic a lack of students/traffic no students/traffic all students/traffic most students/traffic most of the students/traffic other students/traffic

1. *A few* means several and can have a positive meaning, while *few* means almost none or not many and can have a negative meaning.

   *The engineering student took **a few** humanities courses during his first three years at college, so he had **few** humanities courses to take his last year.*

   A few changes its meaning to many by adding *quite*.

   *In the workplace, engineers are required to write **quite a few** reports, so good writing skills are important.*

2. *A little* means some and can have a positive meaning, while *little* means almost none or not enough and can have a negative meaning.

   *The teenager spent **a little** money at the movies; therefore, he had **little** money for dinner afterward.*

WRITING TIP

When using *few* and *little* in writing, it is necessary to provide some background that explains the negative meaning of these two quantifiers.

*Because this problem has just come to the public's attention, **little** information is available on post-traumatic stress disorder (PTSD) in police and firefighters.*

*There has been a lot of concern about soldiers with PTSD, but **few** studies have been done on police and firefighters who experience many of the same problems.*

---

3. The quantifiers *many* and *much* have a general meaning, while the quantifiers *many of the* and *much of the* refer to a specific group.

   Many *medical treatments are accepted overseas before they are widely used in the United States.*

   Many of the *medical treatments for cancer make patients sicker before the patients get better.*

   Much *knowledge is required of medical students.*

   Much of the *knowledge that medical students acquire comes from their patients.*

4. The quantifier *many* occurs in both affirmative and negative statements.

> *The project included* **many** *analyses of the reasons for immigration.*

> *There are* **not many** *statistics on the effects of immigration on family cohesion.*

In contrast, the quantifier *much* is usually used in negative statements but can be used in affirmative statements as well.

> *There is* **not much** *research on the topic of reverse immigration.*

> *There is* **much** *research on the topic of immigration during the early twentieth century.*

WRITING TIP

In formal academic writing, *much* and *many* are more appropriate than *a lot of* and *lots of*. Although these quantifiers have the same meaning, *a lot of* and *lots of* are considered informal. Even more formal than *much* and *many* are *a great deal of* and *a great many*.

---

5. *Much* and *many* can be used as pronouns. A plural verb is needed for *many*, while *much* needs the third person singular verb.

> *Some birds migrate long distances every year.* **Many** *fly north to the Arctic in the spring and return south in the fall.* **Much** *is still not understood about how these birds navigate such long distances.*

6. Use *some* with plural count and uncountable nouns to refer to something in a nonspecific way. Do not use *some* to refer to a noun in general.

> *Information helps people make good decisions.* (refers to *information* in general)

> *The driver's handbook provides* **some** *helpful information.* (refers to *information* that is nonspecific)

> *The driver's handbook presents* **some** *consequences for drinking and driving.* (refers to consequences that are nonspecific)

7. When there is a group of similar items, *another* means one more in addition to those already mentioned. *Other* refers to several more items in addition to the ones already mentioned.

> *The Israelis and the Palestinians have met numerous times over peace negotiations. The two sides have* **another** *meeting next month, which may lead to* **other** *negotiations in the future.*

8. An uncountable noun can be made countable by placing a unit of measure before it.

a piece of *advice*	**a head of** *lettuce*
a bit of *traffic*	**a pound of** *beef*
a glass of *juice*	**a pair of** *pants/jeans/shorts/pajamas/glasses/scissors*
a carton of *milk*	

DEMONSTRATIVE ADJECTIVES

Demonstrative adjectives show distance in time and space. A demonstrative adjective must agree with the noun it modifies in number. Like quantifiers, the demonstrative adjectives *this, that, these,* and *those* pair with count and uncountable nouns. Study how the demonstrative adjectives pair with nouns in the following chart.

	COUNT NOUNS		UNCOUNTABLE NOUNS
	SINGULAR	PLURAL	
Near in time or space	this	these	this
Distant in time or space	that	those	that

1. The demonstrative adjectives *this* and *these* show a small distance in space from the present location, while *that* and *those* show a large distance in space from the present location.

   This *classroom where we are standing is freezing cold, while* **that** *classroom down the hall is boiling hot.*

   Those *students down the hall are uncomfortably hot, while* **these** *students in our classroom are very cold.*

2. The demonstrative adjectives *this* and *these* show a period of time that is closer to the present time, while *that* and *those* show a period of time that is more distant from the present time.

   This *current research is much more accurate than* **that** *older information.*

   These *studies from last month show different results than* **those** *investigations from last year.*

3. Demonstrative adjectives can function as pronouns if the nouns they refer to are clear. *This* and *that* use a singular verb, while *these* and *those* use a plural verb.

   Chlorine and vinegar should not be mixed. **This** *(the mixture) causes a negative chemical reaction, but* **those** *(chlorine and vinegar) are safe chemicals when not combined.*

WRITING TIP

In writing, the distance in time and space is not always clear, so either *this/that* or *these/those* may be appropriate. Use a demonstrative adjective in a piece of writing only when the noun it refers to has been mentioned before.

It rained heavily in the Australian northeast last month, causing a vast flood in that area. **This flood** *caused millions in losses for the Australian economy.*

not *It rained heavily in the Australian northeast last month. This flood caused millions in losses for the Australian economy.*

POSSESSIVES

Adjectives

The possessive adjectives are *my, your, his, her, its, one's, our,* and *their*. Possessive adjectives can be used with singular or plural nouns, but they must agree in gender (male, female, or neuter) with the noun that they refer to.

President Jimmy Carter started **his** nonprofit organization, The Carter Center, in 1982.

The Carter Center accomplishes **its** mission with the help of many volunteers.

President and Mrs. Carter work to accomplish **their** goal of ending human suffering by improving human rights.

WRITING TIP

The possessive adjective *one's* is very formal in American English. Writers generally use *his or her, his, her,* or *their* rather than *one's*.

Very formal:	*One should consider one's goals before choosing a career path.*
Preferred:	*One should consider his or her goals before choosing a career path.*
Acceptable:	*One should consider his goals before choosing a career path.*
Acceptable:	*One should consider her goals before choosing a career path.*
Most common:	*People should consider their goals before choosing a career path.*

Nouns

Another way to show possession is to use the possessive *'s*. In the following chart, study how the apostrophe is used with singular and plural nouns to show ownership.

	SINGULAR POSSESSIVE	PLURAL POSSESSIVE
Regular nouns	a student's book	the students' books
Irregular nouns	a woman's office	the women's offices
Words that end in –*s* or an *s*-like sound	a genius's test score *or* a genius' test score an ax's handle France's exports	the geniuses' test scores the axes' handles
Words that end in –*ss*	a business's balance sheet *or* a business' balance sheet	the businesses' balance sheets

1. The possessive *'s* is generally used only with human or animate objects.

a child's toy

a dog's bowl

not *a house's roof*

2. When there is joint ownership, the possessive *'s* is attached to only the second noun.

> *France and England's trade agreement will be signed next month.*

When there is individual ownership, the possessive *'s* is attached to both nouns.

> *France's and England's agricultural exports have been rising.*

3. The *'s* can also be used when letters or numbers are difficult to read without the apostrophe.

> *The spelling of Mississippi has four i's, four s's, and two p's.*
>
> *The television series is on ten DVD's (or DVDs).*
>
> *Big band music was popular during the 1940's (or 1940s).*

NUMBERS

1. A cardinal number shows how many of something there are. Cardinal numbers are 1, 2, 3, and so on. Cardinal numbers below 10 are generally spelled out.

> *Michigan held **two** elections last year.*
>
> *More than **100** propositions appeared on ballots in the last **nine** years.*

2. An ordinal number shows the order of something in time or location. Ordinal numbers are first, second, third, and so on. Ordinal numbers below 10 are generally spelled out.

> *The **fourth** proposition was on increasing the driving age, and the **11th** proposition was on revising the State Constitution.*

Self Check 2

Circle the sentence that uses determiners correctly.

1. (a) Goddess is said to protect the island of Miyajima in Japan.

   (b) A goddess is said to protect the island of Miyajima in Japan.

2. (a) Only a few coal and steam trains remain; most are now electric.

   (b) Only quite a few coal and steam trains remain; most are now electric.

3. (a) Some scholars call math the universal language. This belief comes from the fact that math does not change from country to country.

   (b) Some scholars call math the universal language. These belief comes from the fact that math does not change from country to country.

4. (a) Athena, the Greek goddess of wisdom, is said to have come from the head of his father.

   (b) Athena, the Greek goddess of wisdom, is said to have come from the head of her father.

5. (a) Today the bosses office is the same as all other offices.

   (b) Today the boss's office is the same as all other offices.

EDITING PRACTICE

1. *Put a check (✓) next to the sentences that use nouns and determiners correctly. Correct the sentences that have errors. There may be more than one way to correct some errors.*

_____ **1.** Dermatologists suggest that one stay out of the sun especially if one's skin is fair.

_____ **2.** Weakened tooth enamel can lead to a great number of cavities. Many occur even when patients brush and floss regularly.

_____ **3.** Many of climate researchers in California warn that the state may have a "superstorm" that could cause billions in damages.

_____ **4.** The doctors are beginning to recommend homeopathic remedies for common illnesses.

_____ **5.** The China has surpassed the Japan as the second largest manufacturing country in the world.

_____ **6.** Many modern skyscrapers are made of glasses.

_____ **7.** The jury in courtroom number 12 disagree over the final verdict.

_____ **8.** Those who love language should study the linguistics.

_____ **9.** Driving is not recommended during dangerous weathers, including heavy fogs, sleets, and snows.

_____ **10.** The major U.S. financial indices include the Dow Jones, NASDAQ, S&P, and New York Stock Exchange.

_____ **11.** The audition for the upcoming musical will require one monologue and six musical bars of a song to demonstrate both acting and singing abilities.

_____ **12.** Canada has ten provinces and three territories within their borders.

_____ **13.** The families assets are protected so others do not have access to them.

_____ **14.** The citizens of St. Louis passed 2 laws that will ban puppy mills in the city.

2. Read the following paragraph. Complete the paragraph by circling the correct nouns and determiners.

World War I and World War II were unlike _____

                          1. other / another

wars of the past or present. _____ were total wars. Not

                  2. These / This

only were countries all over the globe involved in battles and struggles, but

all _____ of the countries and nations were involved as

      3. part / parts

well. _____ wars took priority economically, politically,

       4. Ø / The

and socially. Everyone became _____ patriot to his or

              5. a / the

her country and _____ allies. Total war took a toll on all

        6. its / their

parties, both military and civilian, on the battle lines and the homefront.

Total war meant no restrictions on both civilians and combatants; there

was fear that this kind of war could annihilate the entire world as well as

all of _____. Unlike previous wars in which fighting

     7. humanities / humanity

was generally for material gain or conquest, countries that entered into

World Wars I and II were fighting for their very existence. If they did

not enter into the _____, countries could likely have

       8. fighting / fightings

their _____ taken away from them by others who

   9. sovereignty / sovereignties

wished to dominate their lands and their people. As the concentration

camps of World War II show us, countries could imprison people with

_____ motivation other than their hatred for people of

   10. little / a little

certain racial backgrounds. For these reasons, World War I and World War II

were unique in their all-encompassing nature.

3. In the following paragraph, the underlined nouns and determiners have errors. Write your corrections above each error. There may be more than one way to correct some errors.

When we discuss the accomplishments of explorers, we may think, first, of the twentieth-century New Zealand mountaineers, Sir Edmund Hillary. However, to gain a true appreciation of their accomplishments, it is important to understand that Hillary also experienced failures in his climbing career before his successful summit of Mount Everest in 1953. One of these failures was noted in Hillarys 1951 attempt to climb Cho Oyu.

After a success of his climb of Mount Everest, Sir Hillary also reached the South Pole overland in 1958. Hillary capped his career in 1985 with astronaut Neil Armstrong by flying over Arctic Ocean and landing at the North Pole, making him a first person to reach both poles and the summit of Everest.

Sir Edmund Hillary became a accomplished philanthropist. In 1960s he focused his efforts on protecting the environments and in helping the Nepalese people by building clinics, hospitals, and school. His environmental work was influential in convincing Nepalese government to declare the area surrounding Mount Everest the national park. Queen Elizabeth II knighted Edmund Hillary as a Knight of the Order of the Garter in 1995. He died on January 11, 2008, at 88 years old.

4. *The following paragraph has ten errors with nouns and determiners. Find and correct the errors. Use your dictionary for unfamiliar vocabulary. There may be more than one way to correct some errors.*

When the French Revolution began in 1789, it represented hope, equality, and freedom for many British writer. They respected and admired the way the French population was rebelling against the countries monarchy and hierarchical rule. Both the British and French hoped this rebellion was the dawns of freedom for every person, from a lowliest beggar to the wealthiest tradesman. The French Revolution inspired British writers to reflect on one's own system of rule and social structure. It was a time of hopefulness, idealism, and youth; however, these wonderful feelings did not last, nor did the French Revolution. The infamous Reign of Terror followed and killed all hope. The Reign of Terror produced a kind of backlashes against that British writers who had supported the Revolution. For an up-and-coming writers of the nineteenth century, the French Revolution represented a break from the past, which seemed too strict, too caught up in hierarchies and etiquette. These writers welcomed revolutionary ideas and social disorders as breaks from the past and looked toward the France as a beacon of hope even though the Revolution did not result in the hoped-for changes of the time.

WRITING TOPICS

Most academic essays and research papers require an introduction with a strong thesis statement. The body paragraphs following the introduction support the thesis with references to outside sources. These outside sources might be summarized, quoted, or paraphrased. Notice how the following body paragraph, which was taken from a longer piece of writing, includes a topic sentence, a body with support from outside sources, and a concluding sentence. Use this paragraph as a model when you write about one of the following topics.

Study how the writer of the following paragraph uses nouns and determiners. Circle an example of each kind of noun and determiner presented in this chapter: a count and an uncountable noun, an indefinite and a definite article, Ø article, a quantifier, a demonstrative adjective, a possessive adjective, a possessive noun, and a number.

It has often been said that if people believe they can do something, they will be able to do it, and if they believe they cannot do something, they won't. In addition, some argue that becoming overly emotional can trigger a negative or positive response in our bodies. Are such beliefs true? Can our mind truly alter our body and abilities? This is one idea that noetic science is trying to prove. According to the noetic sciences' official Web site, the "essential hypothesis underlying the noetic sciences is simply that *consciousness* matters."[1] With this belief that our minds affect our health, a new school of medicine is emerging. It is "whole-being" centered rather than disease centered, as most medical practices are today. Some researchers in the noetic sciences say that the placebo effect is a perfect example of how our minds affect our bodies. The placebo effect states that a patient's belief in a medical pill or treatment allows him or her to overcome a medical condition. The patient's mind, not the medicine, allows him or her to get better. This is the idea behind noetic science. It is quite possible that, in years to come, the whole-being approach to medicine may become as prevalent as today's disease-centered approach to medicine.

Choose one of the topics below and write at least one paragraph. Find an outside source to support the ideas that you present in your writing. After you complete your first draft, concentrate on editing your work. Keep in mind the editing practice from this chapter.

1. Many people believe that "A healthy body makes a healthy mind." Explain why this popular saying is true and how one can accomplish it.

2. Use your own words to define the term *independence*. Explain why independence is important and why so many wars have been fought over it.

Go to page 172 for more practice with nouns and determiners.

---

[1] "What Are the Noetic Sciences?" Institute of Noetic Sciences, accessed July 14, 2011, http://noetic.org/about/what-are-noetic-sciences/.

Agreement

GRAMMAR FOCUS

Subject-verb agreement and pronoun agreement are necessary within sentences, paragraphs, and longer pieces of writing. In this chapter, subject-verb agreement rules for fractions, percentages, correlative conjunctions, and collective nouns are reviewed. Pronoun agreement is another area where further study and practice will allow you to write cohesively by providing links within sentences, paragraphs, and essays. Notice how the following sentences use pronouns to link the idea from the first sentence to the ideas in the second sentence.

> **Sea kelp,** also known as seaweed, has been an important part of the Japanese diet for centuries. **This** is because **it** has high concentrations of vitamins and minerals, and the sea surrounding Japan has abundant supplies of **it**.

Pretest

Check your understanding of agreement. Put a check (✓) next to the sentences that are correct.

_____ **1.** A number of the results are inconclusive.

_____ **2.** Employers and employees often disagree when they demand a change in work benefits.

_____ **3.** The number of affirmative votes are higher than the number of negative votes.

_____ **4.** Half of the experiments were completed.

_____ **5.** Police officers may question a person if they act suspiciously.

_____ **6.** Five kilometers are the distance between point A and point B.

_____ **7.** None of the equations have known variables.

_____ **8.** Mathematics as well as economics requires good analytical skills.

_____ **9.** Civil rights legislation that was passed in earlier decades have remained important to this day.

_____ **10.** The class must submit its papers before the midnight deadline.

Notice how both subject-verb agreement and pronoun agreement are used in the following paragraph. Some pronouns are underlined once. Circle the nouns that the underlined pronouns refer to. In addition, some nouns are underlined twice. Circle the verbs that agree with the nouns that are underlined twice.

Robots first appeared in ancient myths and legends and have continued to appear in modern literature and movies, but exactly how have <u>they</u> been used in real life? Beginning with the Greeks in 200 B.C. <u>a number</u> of tasks have been performed with robots, but one of the most successful modern uses of robots is robotic surgery. A surgeon works on a patient from a remote location, using foot pedals and hand controllers to operate a camera and robotic arms that are inserted in the patient. <u>This</u> gives the surgeon control of ultrafine tissues that <u>he or she</u> does not have with the human hand. Robotic <u>equipment</u> is ideal for pediatric, neurological, and vascular surgery, which all require microscopic work. Because the incisions are so small with robotic surgery, <u>pain as well as scarring</u> is lessened, leading to a faster recovery time for most patients. However, robotic systems and training are expensive. Over <u>1.2 million dollars</u> is the estimated cost of a surgical robot. While robots were originally the creations of myths and legends, today <u>they</u> assist humans in some of the most advanced procedures in medical science.

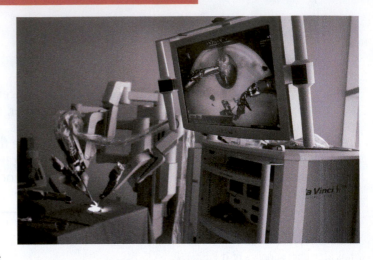

RULES FOR SUBJECT-VERB AGREEMENT

1. A verb must agree with its subject.

In the present, add an *–s* ending to most verbs that follow third-person singular subjects.

*Nina's younger sister live**s** on campus in the dorm. Nina's older sisters live in different locations on campus.*

*In many cultures, one leave**s** home for the first time at marriage.*

*The U.S. Congress does not enforce the laws of the country; it create**s** the laws of the country.*

WRITING TIP

When using the third-person singular in the present, remember the "one *–s* rule": the *–s* is on either the subject or the verb, not both.

*Tree**s** improve the natural environment.*

*A tree improve**s** the natural environment.*

2. The subject and verb must agree in sentences when adjective clauses or prepositional phrases separate the subject and verb.

*An ethical **question** that has been unresolved for many centuries **is** still likely to cause disagreement today.*

*The **rules** that children learn at home **need** to be reinforced at school.*

Campsites *near the river* **cost** *more than those by the road.*

One *of the entrance exams* **is** *harder than the others.*

3. *A number of* and *the number of* follow different subject-verb agreement rules. A plural verb always follows *a number of* while a singular verb always follows *the number of*.

A number of *different equations* **solve** *the problem.*

The number of *equations* **varies** *with each problem.*

4. Percentages, fractions, amounts, and distances are followed by singular verbs.

Thirty-seven percent is *the correct answer.*

One-third *nearly* **equals** *.33.*

Ten dollars makes *the total $100.*

Twenty-six miles and 385 yards is *a marathon.*

Percentages, fractions, amounts, and distances followed by an *of* phrase require that the verb agree with the noun closest to it.

Thirty-three percent of the <u>test</u> <u>is</u> *difficult; therefore,* **two-thirds of the <u>questions</u> <u>are</u>** *easy.*

Since **10 kilometers of the <u>race</u> <u>goes</u>** *through downtown,* **20 percent of the <u>entry fees</u> <u>go</u>** *to the downtown police department.*

5. *None* is followed by a singular verb.

A: *Has it snowed this winter?*

B: **None has** *fallen yet.*

None + of phrase is followed by a singular verb even if the phrase is plural.

<u>None of</u> the results <u>is</u> *complete.*

NOTE: In conversational or informal English, the verb generally agrees with the noun closest to it in sentences that use *none*.

Informal/Conversational: **None of the <u>injuries</u> <u>are</u>** *life threatening.*

6. The noun and the verb closest to each other must agree in sentences with the correlative conjunctions *neither/nor, either/or,* and *not only/but also.*

Neither *the results* **nor the <u>experiment</u> is** *complete.*

Either *the head researcher* **or the lab <u>assistants</u> <u>plan</u>** *to write up the test results.*

Not only *Americans and Canadians* **but also <u>Australians</u> <u>speak</u>** *English as a first language.*

NOTE: Neither/nor is normally used only in formal academic writing.

WRITING TIP

Correlative conjunctions make your writing sound academic and formal. Along with the use of academic vocabulary, these conjunctions can change an ordinary sentence into one that has greater impact.

Spain and Ireland cannot get away from their debt crisis.

Neither *Spain* **nor** *Ireland is able to escape their debt crisis.*

7. The subject and verb must agree in sentences with the compound prepositions *as well as, together with, in addition to,* and *along with.*

Confidence, as well as humility, **is** important in political leaders.

Temperament, in addition to emotions, **plays** an important part in the decisions that people make.

Compassion, together with many friendships, **makes** a happy life.

Strong **relationships, along with** satisfying employment, **lead** to contentment in life.

8. When a word is omitted but understood from a previous clause, the verb must agree with the omitted word.

The East Coast schools have better reputations than **the West's do**. (the West's refers to the West Coast schools)

Well-researched papers get better grades than **the quickly written do**. (the quickly written = the quickly written papers)

9. Collective nouns are generally used with singular verbs because the group functions as one unit. However, when the members of the group function as individuals, a plural verb is used. Some common collective nouns include *audience, band, class, committee, couple, crowd, faculty, family, gang, government, group, jury, the media, orchestra, the public, staff,* and *team.*

The **class studies** several theories each week.

The **class have** differing viewpoints on the best theory to apply.

Some collective nouns have to be followed by plural verbs. These include *the military police, the poor, the rich, the old, the young, the elderly,* and other collective nouns that come from adjectives that describe people.

The elderly are valued in many cultures.

The young are an important group for advertisers.

10. When the subject of a sentence is a clause, the verb is singular. This is true even if the clause has plural nouns.

What the research finds is controversial. [singular subject = *What the research finds*]

When the flowers bloom depends on the weather. [singular subject = *When the flowers bloom*]

Self Check 1

Circle the sentence that uses subject-verb agreement correctly.

1. **(a)** None of the results are thoroughly explained.

   (b) None of the results is thoroughly explained.

2. **(a)** Fish, in addition to fruits, vegetables, and grains, composes a healthy diet.

   (b) Fish, in addition to fruits, vegetables, and grains, compose a healthy diet.

3. **(a)** The number of cancer studies have decreased in recent years.

   (b) The number of cancer studies has decreased in recent years.

4. (a) Applied linguistics, which investigates real-life language issues, includes the fields of psychology, anthropology, and sociology.

   (b) Applied linguistics, which investigates real-life language issues, include the fields of psychology, anthropology, and sociology.

5. (a) The poor frequently lives in substandard housing.

   (b) The poor frequently live in substandard housing.

RULES FOR PRONOUN AGREEMENT

1. A personal pronoun must agree with the noun it refers to.

> **Analysis** *requires logical thinking.* **It** *also requires creativity.*

> *Most* **internships** *are unpaid because* **they** *give students valuable professional experience in place of money.*

Traditionally, masculine pronouns were used.

> *An* **engineer** *must communicate well.* **He** *must also behave ethically.*

Frequently today, both masculine and feminine pronouns are used.

> *A* **journalist** *must be a good writer; however,* **he or she** *must also speak clearly.*

2. In formal academic writing, singular pronouns (*he, she, it, his, her,* etc.) are used to refer to the indefinite pronouns *everybody, everyone, everything, somebody, someone, something, anybody, anyone, anything, nobody, no one,* and *nothing.*

> **Everyone** *must show identification before* **he or she** *can enter an airplane.*

In informal English, it is acceptable to use plural pronouns to refer to indefinite pronouns.

> **Nobody** *who shows* **their** *identification will be questioned further.*

3. Use a singular pronoun (*it* or *its*) when a collective noun refers to a single unit or group.

> *The* **committee** *evaluated the scholarship applications.* **It** *awarded ten large scholarships.* (*It* refers to the committee as a single unit.)

Use a plural pronoun (*they, them,* or *their*) when a collective noun refers to individuals in the group.

> *My* **family** *still lives in the Northeast, but* **they** *moved to different cities in the region after college.* (*They* refers to individuals in the family, not the family as a group.)

USING PRONOUN AGREEMENT

1. Use pronouns such as *it, they,* and *them* to link the ideas within your writing and avoid repetition. Pronouns refer back to previously stated information.

> **Climate change** *affects all countries throughout the world. Therefore,* **it** *is an important area of worldwide research.*

> *New* **international laws** *are effective in slowing climate change, but not all countries have agreed to* **them**.

2. Use the singular pronoun *it* or *this* to refer back to an entire clause or sentence.

> *Many studies show that drinking a moderate amount of wine is healthful.* **This** *has resulted in increased wine sales. (It/This refers to the entire first sentence.)*

3. The demonstrative pronouns *this, that, these,* and *those* also refer back to previously stated information. *This* and *that* refer to singular nouns, while *these* and *those* refer to plural nouns.

> *Greenhouse gases are trapped in the earth's atmosphere.* **These** *prevent heat from escaping into space. (These refer to greenhouse gases.)*

> *The burning of fossil fuels increases the poisonous gases in the air.* **It** *has been evident since the Industrial Revolution. (It refers to the burning of fossil fuels.)*

4. *This, that, these,* and *those* can also be used as demonstrative adjectives to refer back to previously stated information.

> *Carbon emissions are directly related to energy consumption.* **These** *emissions create the greenhouse effect. If we do not slow* **this** *energy consumption, the earth's temperature will continue to rise.*

5. Using pronouns can sometimes create an ambiguous statement. Do not use a pronoun if it is not clear who or what the pronoun refers to.

> Ambiguous: *When students evaluate their professors,* **they** *usually learn a lot from* **their** *responses. (It is not clear whether they and their refer to the students or the professors.)*

> Clear: *When students evaluate their professors,* **the professors** *usually learn a lot from* **the students'** *responses.*

6. *You* and *one* can both be used as impersonal pronouns; however, *you* is more informal than *one*. Use *you* in spoken or informal English and *one* for formal or academic writing.

> Informal: *To get good grades,* **you** *should study a lot.*

> Formal: *Confidence is important for* **one** *to succeed in life.*

WRITING TIP

Several different possessive adjectives may be used to refer to *one*.

Very formal:	*One must invest for one's future.*
Preferred:	*One must invest for his or her future.*
Acceptable:	*One must invest for his future.* Or: *One must invest for her future.*
Unacceptable:	*One must invest for your future.*

Self Check 2

Circle the sentence that uses pronoun agreement correctly.

1. (a) If parents discuss chores with their children, the children usually get mad.

   (b) If parents discuss chores with their children, they usually get mad.

2. (a) China has the greatest number of cell phone users in the world. They are followed by India and the European Union.

   (b) China has the greatest number of cell phone users in the world. It is followed by India and the European Union.

3. (a) Benjamin Franklin said that one will have no gain unless he or she has pain.

(b) Benjamin Franklin said that one will have no gain unless you have pain.

4. (a) Everyone must finish the competition before they receive an award.

(b) Everyone must finish the competition before he or she receives an award.

5. (a) Taking exams raises people's blood pressure because it is a stressful experience.

(b) Taking exams raises people's blood pressure because they are a stressful experience.

EDITING PRACTICE

1. *Put a check (✓) next to the sentences that use subject-verb agreement and pronoun agreement correctly. Correct the sentences that have errors.*

_____ **1.** Journalists who report from a war zone often experiences post-traumatic stress disorder just like soldiers.

_____ **2.** Developing leadership skills helps one achieve success in their life.

_____ **3.** When the government raises taxes, they should also improve services.

_____ **4.** The faculty meets every month on the second Tuesday.

_____ **5.** The difference between popular magazines and scholarly journals is that they are academic and aimed at professionals in the field.

_____ **6.** None of Misoo's children is able to speak English fluently.

_____ **7.** Over the past few years, textbook prices have risen faster than the prices of similar products. This has led to several federal investigations.

_____ **8.** Sixty percent is the lowest passing score.

_____ **9.** Everyone in law school must pass the state bar exam before they can practice law.

_____ **10.** An effective CEO should regularly communicate with his or her subordinates.

_____ **11.** Fifty dollars belong to the seller of each product.

_____ **12.** Where crimes have significantly decreased are in the inner city.

_____ **13.** Throughout the world, wedding ceremonies are joyous occasions, but they also teach us a lot about a culture's values.

_____ **14.** Real estate foreclosures, along with declining employment, has slowed the world economy.

_____ **15.** Not only the coach but also the players are happy with the team's results.

2. *Read the following paragraph. Complete the paragraph by circling the answer that uses agreement correctly.*

When people work without financial

or material gain, _____
1. he or she is / they are

volunteering. They do _____ to
2. this / these

promote decency and improve the quality of life

for others. _____ also allows
3. This / They

the volunteers to gain valuable skills. However,

some volunteers in areas such as education,

medicine, and law already _____
4. has / have

advanced skills. All types of volunteerism

_____ society in several ways. First of all, volunteering
5. benefits / benefit

has economic benefits. Governments and private businesses do not have to

pay for the work that volunteers do; therefore, a country gains economically

by reducing the money that the government _____. It is
6. spends / spend

estimated that as much as $500 _____ saved per work hour
7. is / are

when skilled workers volunteer _____ time. Social benefits
8. his or her / their

of volunteerism, in addition to the economic benefit, _____
9. includes / include

building united and stable communities where the citizens trust one another.

Personal benefits are also gained through volunteering. Meeting new people

and learning new work skills are just two. By looking at all the rewards of

volunteering, it is clear that volunteers reap more rewards that those who

_____.
10. does not / do not

3. *In the following paragraph, five of the underlined words, phrases, or clauses have agreement errors. Write your corrections above each error.*

Crime, poverty, drugs, racism, and the environment are all serious societal problems, but many Americans rank the decline in ethics as a greater problem than <u>this</u>. As evidence of an ethical decline, 58.3 percent of high
<u>   1</u>
school students said they had allowed someone to copy their work in 1969, while more recently 97 percent <u>have admitted</u> the same. According to
<u>   2</u>
plagiarism.org, of all college and university students, over three-quarters <u>admit</u> cheating at least one time. Cheating, which still includes old-style
<u> 3</u>
methods such as using crib notes (a small piece of paper with answers that a student secretly looks at during an exam), whispering answers, and copying homework, <u>has become</u> much more advanced with the advent of computers,
<u>   4</u>
smart phones, and advanced calculators. Further evidence of ethical concerns <u>are</u> the incidence of plagiarism in our high schools, colleges, and <u>universities</u>.
<u>5</u>
Thirty-six percent of college students <u>admit</u> that they have plagiarized written
<u>   6</u>
written material. That cheaters rarely get caught <u>is</u> the main reason cheating is
<u>   7</u>
on the rise according to the majority of students interviewed. Many faculty <u>feels</u> that nothing <u>is done</u> by school officials to stop or slow cheating in
<u>8</u>   <u>9</u>
general and plagiarism in particular. Students have many excuses for their cheating: the need for success, lack of time and interest, and unclear standards. However, none of these excuses <u>is comforting</u> for those concerned
<u>   10</u>
about an ethical decline in society.

4. *The following paragraph has ten agreement errors. Find and correct the errors.*

Pets play important roles throughout people's lives; however, it is with the elderly that pets can have the most positive effects. One of the many benefits of pets are the heightened self-worth that the elderly feels by having something to look after and to feel responsible for. Loneliness as well as isolation often accompany old age. This is diminished because of the need to feed, clean, and exercise a pet. These responsibilities also reduces absent-mindedness and confusion that are common in old age. Not only mental capability but also physical activity are improved because of a pet. A number of international research studies shows that pets help the elderly fight against apathy as well as indifference. Another benefit is the safety that a pet provides if their owner lives alone. Overall, pets help senior citizens remain interested and active in life, which leads to more human contact for them. Of all the research done on pets and the elderly, none show any negative consequences of pet ownership. What the numerous studies overwhelmingly prove are the benefits of having the companionship of an animal, especially in old age.

WRITING TOPICS

Most academic essays and research papers require an introduction with a strong thesis statement. The body paragraphs following the introduction support the thesis with references to outside sources. These outside sources might be summarized, quoted, or paraphrased. Notice how the following body paragraph, which was taken from a longer piece of writing, includes a topic sentence, a body with support from outside sources, and a concluding sentence. Use this paragraph as a model when you write about one of the following topics.

Study the agreement in the following student paragraph. Locate and circle examples of the kinds of agreement that you studied in this chapter.

One problem associated with video games is increased aggression in children. Anne Harding reports in "Violent Games Linked to Child Aggression" that some studies show that "virtual violence in these games may make kids more aggressive in real life."[1] Although it is difficult to know if violent games make children more aggressive or if aggressive children are attracted to violent games, recent studies have tried to address this question. Children who were exposed to more video-game violence showed more violent behavior such as hitting, kicking, or getting into fights than their peers who were not exposed to as much violent game content. This may be because children who play a lot of violent games begin to believe that the world is a violent place and that the only way to handle this is with aggression. Another theory reported by Harding comes from Dr. L. Rowell Huesmann, director of the Research Center for Group Dynamics at the University of Michigan. He asserts that children "become desensitized to violence."[2] In other words, children eventually become numb to violence, which makes it easier to participate in. Although not everyone is convinced that violent games lead to aggressive behavior, more research is pointing in this direction.

Choose one of the topics below and write at least one paragraph. Find an outside source to support the ideas that you present in your writing. Use a variety of subjects and pronouns that require careful agreement. After you complete your first draft, concentrate on editing your work. Keep in mind the editing practice from this chapter.

1. Computer games have become very popular over the past several decades. Many teenagers as well as adults love gaming, but some people believe that there are problems associated with it. Write about the benefits and/or challenges associated with the use of computer games.

2. A college education is the most important goal for many people, while others feel that gaining real-life experience is more valuable than book learning. Explain why book learning or life experience is more important for success in life.

Go to page 175 for more practice with agreement.

....

[1] Anne Harding, "Violent Video Games Linked to Child Aggression," *Health Magazine,* 2009, http://www.cnn.com/2008/HEALTH/family/11/03/healthmag.violent.video.kids/.

[2] Harding, "Violent Video Games."

6

Conditionals

GRAMMAR FOCUS

Conditional sentences occur in many types of writing, including expository, scientific, and mathematical. To use conditional sentences well, writers need a good understanding of not only complex sentence structure, verb tenses, and modals but also the subtle meanings in unreal or hypothetical situations. Notice how the following three sentences use similar forms but convey very different meanings because of the use of the conditional.

FACTUAL	Today we know that if an animal has a small brain, it may still be highly intelligent.
HYPOTHETICAL	If we compared an animal's brain size at birth and as an adult, we could learn about its ability to learn.
COUNTERFACTUAL	Even if dinosaurs had developed large brains, they might not have been intelligent animals.

Pretest

Check your understanding of conditionals. Put a check (✓) next to the sentences that are correct.

_____ **1.** If a vehicle runs out of coolant, it will likely overheat.

_____ **2.** Only if a marriage license is granted, will the marriage be legal.

_____ **3.** Fat cells will be remained even if a person loses weight.

_____ **4.** Special-interest groups such as the oil and gas industry hope that new laws didn't limit their access to important legislators.

_____ **5.** Had scientists understood DNA earlier, we would have seen more medical advances today.

_____ **6.** If global warming were to slow, ocean levels would not rise as has been predicted.

_____ **7.** The United States didn't enter World War II if Pearl Harbor had not been attacked.

_____ **8.** If the environmentalists should happen to stop the deforestation of the Brazilian rainforest, millions of animals would have remained in a suitable habitat.

_____ **9.** The American Medical Association wishes that lawsuits had not caused malpractice insurance to increase so dramatically.

_____ **10.** The courts issue heavy fines whenever citations were not paid by the due date.

Notice how the following paragraph uses conditional sentences. Underline the four sentences that use conditional forms and circle the verbs in each of these sentences.

A stutter occurs if a speaker has difficulty speaking and repeats one sound uncontrollably. This kind of break or interruption in the flow of speech is also called dysfluency. Generally, it occurs on the first consonant in a word, forming a sound such as "Illlike" or "li-li-like." Approximately one percent of the worldwide population has long-term stuttering problems. Unless these people seek help from a professional such as a speech language pathologist, it is unlikely their dysfluency will disappear. Even if they receive professional help, stuttering is frequently a lifelong problem. Nevertheless, there are many famous people who have had huge successes despite having a stutter: Thomas Jefferson, the third U.S. president; James Earl Jones, who is Darth Vader in *Star Wars;* and King George VI of England. As with all people who have a problem, if these people had not worked tirelessly to overcome their problem, they would not have experienced success.

FORMING CONDITIONALS

1. Conditional sentences are complex sentences with two clauses: dependent and independent. The dependent *if* clause states the condition, and the independent or main clause states the result. A conditional sentence can begin with either clause; however, a comma is needed to separate the two clauses if the sentence begins with the dependent *if* clause.

   dependent clause/condition

   If adults experience hearing loss between 41 and 55 decibels,

   independent clause/result

   they have moderate hearing impairment.

   independent clause/result

   Children have mild hearing impairment

   dependent clause/condition

   if they experience hearing loss between 20 and 40 decibels.

2. Conditional sentences are formed with the subordinating conjunctions *if, even if, only if, when, whenever, whether or not,* and *unless.*

3. Conditional sentences are formed in the present, past, and future time frames and can be factual, hypothetical (imaginative), or counterfactual (untrue or unreal).

Conditionals in the Present

TYPE OF CONDITIONAL	FORMING THE CONDITIONAL	EXAMPLE SENTENCE	EXPLANATION
Factual conditionals	*If* clause: simple present Result clause: simple present	Dieters **lose** one pound per week if they **reduce** their consumption by 10 percent. (a scientific fact) If Professor Lipton **gives** an exam, he **holds** a study session the night before. (the professor's habit)	Factual conditionals in the present refer to actions or situations that are facts or habits.
Hypothetical conditionals	*If* clause: simple past Result clause: *would* + base verb	If the college **had** the funding, it **would build** a new library. (In reality, the college does not have enough money, so it cannot build a new library.)	Hypothetical conditionals in the present refer to actions or situations that are unlikely to happen at the present time.
Counterfactual conditionals	*If* clause: simple past Result clause: *would* + base verb	If Martin Luther King, Jr. **were** alive today, he **would** still **be** the leader of the civil rights movement. (In reality, Martin Luther King, Jr. is no longer alive, so he cannot lead the civil rights movement.)	Counterfactual conditionals in the present refer to actions or situations that are untrue at the present time.

NOTE: Hypothetical and counterfactual conditionals in the present are formed in the same way; however, hypothetical conditionals have the possibility of happening while counterfactual conditionals have no possibility of happening.

Conditionals in the Past

TYPE OF CONDITIONAL	FORMING THE CONDITIONAL	EXAMPLE SENTENCE	EXPLANATION
Factual conditionals in the past	*If* clause: simple past Result clause: simple past	In the sixteenth century, people believed that if the moon **was** full, werewolves **were** present. (a true belief in the past) If King George VI of Britain **spoke** publicly, he always **had** his speech therapist by his side. (King George VI's habit)	Factual conditionals in the past refer to actions or situations that were past truths or habits.
Counterfactual conditionals in the past	*If* clause: past perfect Result clause: *would have* + past participle	If the United States **had** not **fought** the Civil War, the northern and southern United States **would have become** separate countries. (In reality, the United States fought the Civil War and remained one country.)	Counterfactual conditionals in the past refer to actions or situations that did not happen or were not true.

Conditionals in the Future

TYPE OF CONDITIONAL	FORMING THE CONDITIONAL	EXAMPLE SENTENCE	EXPLANATION
Future conditionals	*If* clause: simple present Result clause: future (*will* + base verb or *be going to* + base verb)	If Africa **faces** another drought, millions of people **are going to suffer**. (a situation with a strong possibility of happening in the future) Foreign aid **will pour** into Africa during another drought if people **begin** to starve and **migrate** to other regions. (a future plan)	Future conditionals present future plans or situations that are likely to happen under the right conditions.
Hypothetical conditionals in the future	*If* clause: *were* + infinitive Result clause: *would* + base verb	If the college **were to have** the funding, it **would build** a new library. (a weak possibility in the future) If NASA **were to land** astronauts on Mars, the astronauts **would make** many discoveries to help humankind on earth. (a weak future possibility at this time)	Hypothetical conditionals in the future refer to actions or situations that have only a weak possibility of occurring in the future.

Conditionals in Two Time Frames

TYPE OF CONDITIONAL	FORMING THE CONDITIONAL	EXAMPLE SENTENCE	EXPLANATION
Present condition that affects the past	*If* clause: simple past Result clause: *would have* + past participle	If the current president **were** a woman, she **would have helped** women in past elections to win their races. (In reality, the current president is not a woman so was not able to help women win other elections.)	A present situation affects past actions or situations, but in reality neither the present or past situation is true.
Past condition that affects the present	*If* clause: past perfect Result clause: *would* + base verb	If the vaccine **had been** effective, the child **would not be** sick now. (In reality, the vaccine was not effective, so the child is sick now.)	A past action or situation affects the present, but in reality neither the present or past situation is true.

WRITING TIP

In formal academic writing, *were* is used for both singular and plural subjects. *Was* can be used in spoken English and informal writing, but it is not appropriate in most of the writing done at school and work.

Formal: *If the price of oil **were** included in the report, the inflation rate would be eight percent.*

Informal: *If the price of oil **was** included in the report, the inflation rate would be eight percent.*

Self Check 1

Circle the sentence that forms conditionals correctly.

1. **(a)** If the university had the funding, it would gave several more scholarships each year.

   (b) If the university had the funding, it would give several more scholarships each year.

2. (a) If the lab mice take a wrong turn in the maze, the scientists would shock them.

(b) If the lab mice take a wrong turn in the maze, the scientists will shock them.

3. (a) If a hydrogen atom was to bond with other molecules, it would need electrons on the outer ring.

(b) If a hydrogen atom were to bond with other molecules, it would need electrons on the outer ring.

4. (a) The oil spill would have caused less harm, if clean-up crews had used microscopic bacteria to digest the pollutants.

(b) If clean-up crews had used microscopic bacteria to digest the pollutants, the oil spill would have caused less harm.

5. (a) If Congress had approved the president's plan in 1998, the United States would now have a rail line similar to Japan's famous bullet train.

(b) If Congress approved the president's plan in 1998, the United States would now have had a rail line similar to Japan's famous bullet train.

USING CONDITIONALS

1. Modals other than *would* are frequently used in hypothetical and counterfactual conditional sentences. *Would* generally conveys strong certainty, while *may, might, could,* and *should* convey less certainty.

Strong certainty: *If women carried backpacks rather than shoulder bags, they **would have** fewer back problems.*

Less certainty: *If women didn't carry heavy purses, they **might not have** as many back injuries.*

2. There are two ways to weaken a future conditional sentence when the future is not completely certain.

- *May, might, could,* or *should* occur in the result clause of future conditionals when the result is too weak to use *will*.

Certainty: *If more oil is discovered in Alaska, additional oil pipelines **will** crisscross the state.*

Possibility: *If more oil pipelines crisscross Alaska, the natural environment **may** be harmed.*

- *Should, happen to,* or *should happen to* occur in the dependent *if* clause when the condition is only a possibility.

Certainty: *If that country develops a nuclear weapon, it will use the weapon against its neighbors.*

Possibility: *If that country **should** acquire a nuclear weapon, the world community will be alarmed.*

*If that country **happens to** launch a nuclear weapon, the region will become unstable.*

*If other countries **should happen to** retaliate, the world will face a nuclear disaster.*

3. *Should, happen to,* or *should happen to* also weaken present hypothetical conditionals. When these forms are used in the dependent *if* clause, there is little probability of this condition happening.

> *If carmakers* **should** *develop /* **happen to** *develop /* **should happen to** *develop a completely clean car, they would sell millions of cars.*

4. In formal written English, conditional sentences use inverted word order to emphasize that a result is unlikely to happen. This form is possible only when the *if* clause contains the auxiliary verbs *had, should,* or *were.* Delete *if* and switch the position of the subject and auxiliary verb. This is possible in the present, past, and future time frames.

> Present: **If community groups were** *to join in the fight against obesity, the health of our citizens would improve.*
>
> **Were community groups** *to join in the fight against obesity, the health of our citizens would improve.*
>
> Past: **If the United States had not entered** *the Vietnam War, the unrest during the 1960s would have decreased.*
>
> **Had the United States not entered** *the Vietnam War, the unrest during the 1960s would have decreased.*
>
> Future: **If doctors and scientists should find** *a cure for infectious diseases, children around the world would benefit.*
>
> **Should doctors and scientists find** *a cure for infectious diseases, children around the world would benefit.*

5. *When* or *whenever* can be used instead of *if* in factual conditionals in the present and past with no change in meaning.

> *People are more likely to get dementia* **if/when** *they smoke heavily in midlife.*
>
> **When/If** *people had dementia in the past, it was considered a natural part of aging.*

6. *Only if, unless, even if,* and *whether or not* can be used in conditional sentences to make slight changes in meaning.

- *Only if* expresses a unique condition that creates a specific result. No other condition exists to cause this result.

> *Grapes will produce excellent wine* **only if** *the soil they grow in is rich in minerals.*

> When *only if* occurs at the beginning of the sentence, the subject and auxiliary verb change positions in the following independent clause.

> **Only if** *grape vines get sufficient rain* **will they** *produce good wine.*

- *Unless,* like *only if,* expresses a unique condition that creates a specific result. No other condition exists to cause this result. *Unless* and *if . . . not* can often be used in the same way.

> *Medical experiments will continue to use animals* **unless** *the animal rights groups win the battle against their use.*

> *Medical experiments will continue to use animals* **if** *the animal rights groups do* **not** *win the battle against their use.*

- *Even if* expresses a surprising or unexpected result.

> **Even if** *there is a drought, some people continue to water their lawns.*

> *A few people would continue to waste water* **even if** *water levels were dangerously low.*

- *Whether or not* expresses the idea that the condition has no effect on the result; the condition is irrelevant.

  In the business world today, many men are still promoted over women **whether or not** *the men are qualified.*

  Whether or not *women were educated in past generations, they had a difficult time finding good positions in business.*

NOTE: Whether and *or not* can be separated. *Whether* occurs at the beginning of the clause and *or not* occurs at the end of the clause. However, they should not be separated by too many words.

Whether *the medication lowers his blood pressure* **or not**, *he must change his diet.*

not

Whether the medication that he got from his doctor last month and started taking immediately lowers his blood pressure or not, he must change his diet.

WRITING TIP

Whether is more common in written English than *whether or not.*

Written English: **Whether** the job prospects are good or bad, the students must find a summer job.

Spoken English: **Whether or not** the job prospects are good, the students must find a summer job.

---

7. The passive voice is used in conditional sentences under the same circumstances as presented in Chapter 2. The passive voice can occur in the independent clause, dependent clause, or both clauses.

   If the plane **had been flown** *by an inexperienced pilot, all the passengers* **would have been killed** *in the crash.*

8. Negatives can occur in the dependent *if* clause or the independent clause; however, it is preferable to write affirmative conditionals or use a negative in only one clause. When negatives are used in both clauses, the sentence may be unclear.

   If cancer research **does not advance** *quickly, many more people will die at a young age.*

   Even if cancer researchers make new discoveries, some people **may not have** *access to the new procedures and treatments.*

   Unclear: *If the budget meeting had not been canceled, the committee would not be able to make budget decisions today.*

Self Check 2

Circle the sentence that uses conditionals correctly.

1. **(a)** Even if a bill is passed by both the House and the Senate, the president still had the ability to veto it.

   (b) Even if a bill is passed by both the House and the Senate, the president still has the ability to veto it.

2. **(a)** Whether the university adds more classes or increases class size or not, there will still not be enough room for all the students.

   (b) Whether the university adds more classes or increases class size, there will still not be enough room for all the students.

3. (a) Should the government cut funding to the space program, researchers would find it difficult to make new discoveries.

(b) The government should cut funding to the space program if researchers would find it difficult to make new discoveries.

4. (a) When many homes have been foreclosed on by the bank, the value of the surrounding homes drops.

(b) The value of the surrounding homes dropped when many homes have been foreclosed on by the bank.

5. (a) Professional athletes were to accept smaller salaries, their teams would be more profitable.

(b) Were professional athletes to accept smaller salaries, their teams would be more profitable.

WRITING TIP

In formal written English, use *as if* or *as though* instead of *like*. These three conjunctions have the same meaning: in a way that suggests something is true.

Formal: It appears **as if** the fashion industry is recovering from the recession.

Formal: It seems **as though** fashion designers prefer New York to Los Angeles.

Informal: It looks **like** fashion designers are using bright colors this season.

HOPES AND WISHES

Sentences with *wish* and *hope* are similar to conditional sentences. Wishes refer to actions or situations that are the opposite of reality; they are unreal or unlikely. Hopes refer to actions or situations that are possible.

TIME FRAME	FORMING THE SENTENCE	EXAMPLE SENTENCE	EXPLANATION
Present wish	*wish (that)* + simple past or past progressive	High school administrators **wish that** more students **were taking** advanced placement courses. (In reality, not enough high school students take advanced placement classes according to administrators.)	Sentences that express wishes about the present refer to something that is not true or not happening right now.
hope	*hope (that)* + present progressive	The school board **hopes that** the high schools **are offering** enough classes to challenge their students. (At this point, the board does not know whether the high schools are offering enough classes.)	Sentences that express hopes about the present refer to something that is unknown but possible.

(continued on next page)

TIME FRAME	FORMING THE SENTENCE	EXAMPLE SENTENCE	EXPLANATION
Past wish	*wish (that)* + past perfect or *would/could have* + past participle	Many college students **wish that** they **had studied** more in high school. (In reality, these college students did not study much in high school.)	Sentences that express wishes about the past refer to something that did not happen.
hope	*hope (that)* + simple past or present perfect or present perfect progressive	The state **hopes that** schools **have been offering** academic counseling over the past year for all high school students. (At this point, the state is not certain whether academic counseling was offered.)	Sentences that express hopes about the past refer to actions or situations that possibly occurred in the past, but it is not 100 percent certain that they did actually happen.
Future wish	*wish (that)* + *would/could* + base verb	They school district **wishes that** the graduation rate **would improve**. (Graduation rates may improve in the future, but it is not likely.)	Sentences that express wishes about the future refer to something that may happen, but it is less likely than a hope for the future.
hope	*hope (that)* + simple present or future (*will* + base verb or *be going to* + base verb)	The high school **hopes that** over 80 percent of its students **will go** to college.	Sentences that express hopes about the future predict something that has a good possibility of happening.

Self Check 3

Circle the sentence that forms and uses wishes and hopes correctly.

1. **(a)** Most high school students hope that they will be accepted at good universities.

   (b) Most high school students wish that they will be accepted at good universities.

2. **(a)** Many college students wish that they were going to study abroad.

   (b) Many college students wish that they are going to study abroad.

3. **(a)** Parents wish that their teenagers have not been hiding dangerous behaviors from them.

   (b) Parents hope that their teenagers have not been hiding dangerous behaviors from them.

4. **(a)** Fire departments hope that citizens are preparing themselves for possible emergencies.

   (b) Fire departments hope that citizens had prepared themselves for possible emergencies.

5. **(a)** The Green political party wishes that laws currently punished companies more severely for polluting the environment.

   (b) The Green political party hopes that laws currently punished companies more severely for polluting the environment.

EDITING PRACTICE

1. *Put a check (✓) next to the sentences that use conditionals correctly. Correct the sentences that have errors. There may be more than one way to correct some errors.*

_____ **1.** Many people argue that it would be unconstitutional if the government were to ban concealed weapons.

_____ **2.** Einstein frequently paused while talking as if the pauses would help others to understand his ideas.

_____ **3.** Unless homebuyers can make a large down payment, they may have unaffordable monthly payments.

_____ **4.** Most buildings have emergency procedures so that people can safely exit an emergency should occur.

_____ **5.** Sometimes research findings are released even if the findings have not been fully confirmed.

_____ **6.** If birch bark contains properties to lower cholesterol, a new drug would be developed that lowers the rate of heart disease.

_____ **7.** If a driver wants to avoid injury in an accident, he or she might wear a seat belt at all times.

_____ **8.** If annual pay raises were frozen last year, many people could not cope with their rising expenses this year.

_____ **9.** If the food industry policed itself better, many people would not have experienced illnesses caused by food contamination.

_____ **10.** Whether people who are naturally left-handed are more creative in their responses to solving problems or not has been studied by numerous psychologists.

_____ **11.** In the novel by Mark Twain, Huckleberry Finn hopes that he escapes his abusive father by faking his own death and traveling down the Mississippi River.

_____ **12.** Only if drug-sniffing dogs are used in airports, illegal substances and weapons will be detected.

_____ **13.** The CEO wishes that he had chosen a more experienced administrative assistant.

_____ **14.** Companies hope that their sales were growing faster than their competition's.

2. *Read the following paragraph. Complete the paragraph by circling the correct conditional form.*

The earth that we know today was formed millions of years ago as large landmasses, or bodies of land, slowly moved around the earth's surface. During this formation period, whenever large landmasses came together, they

_____,
        1. would fold / fold

creating great mountain ranges. After this type of collision, the two landmasses would have joined together if both

_____ similar types
2. had been composed of / should have been composed of

of rock. However, more times than not, the two landmasses were

made of different rocks with different densities or thicknesses.

Whenever landmasses do not have the same rock density, one mass

_____ the other by pushing upward;
    3. would control / controls

in other words, the pressure from the landmasses that come together is

relieved only if one piece of land _____
                                                 4. pushes / pushed

skyward. This is exactly what happened millions of years ago on

earth. _____ this occurred, rough
        5. Should / Whenever

peaks of land and mountains would form. Depending on the different

circumstances, various rock types were then created. Some types of rocks

can form _____ they are heated to
           6. as if / only if

several hundred degrees Celsius and/or put under high pressure. When large landmasses collided and created pressure, their rubbing together

_____ high levels of heat. Another
       7. causes / would cause

common way that the earth's surface formed was when one landmass

became deeply buried under another landmass. When this happened, huge

volumes of rock _____ in temperature
       8. would increase / will increase

and pressure. This _____ one landmass
       9. should cause / would cause

to rise dramatically while the other was buried deep within the earth.

_____ millions of years
   10. Had these events not occurred / These events had not occurred

ago, we would not have the beauty of huge mountain ranges such as the Alps,

Rockies, and Himalayas today.

3. *In the following paragraph, the underlined verbs are not correct. Correct these errors by writing the correct form above each underlined verb. There may be more than one way to correct some errors.*

    Parenting is a difficult job, and although parents do the best that they

can, most look back and wish that they <u>would do</u> some things differently.
                                   1

Parents know both physical and emotional development is important if their

baby is to grow into a healthy adult. However, some aspects of development

are out of the control of parents. For example, physical development such as

eyesight follows a predictable pattern. If babies are normal at birth, their sight

<u>would be</u> 20/400, which means their near vision is good but their distance
2

vision is limited. Unless a baby <u>had</u> a vision defect, vision should be close to
                                3

20/20 by seven to eight months. When a baby is developing on schedule,

other reflexes and skills <u>would continue</u> to mature. While a baby develops
                      4

physically without much parental influence, emotional development

is an area where parents have greater control. Emotional development

depends on the environment, culture, and people that a baby is exposed to.

For example, if babies <u>were put</u> into a new environment, some adapt very well

5

while others adjust very gradually. This is a result of the emotional bonds or

attachments that babies have already developed. If a baby's parents or

caregivers are always supportive and warm, the baby most likely <u>had developed</u>

6

a "secure bond" and adapts easily in new environments. Only if babies are

secure, <u>they will explore</u> the environment. Even if babies come from

7

supportive environments, some of them <u>should happen to feel</u> insecure in

8

unfamiliar surroundings. Although all parents hope that they <u>were doing</u>

9

everything correctly for their babies' physical and emotional development,

there is not an exact science for raising children. If there <u>was</u>, parents might

10

feel more comfortable with their job of raising children.

4. *The following paragraph has ten errors in the use of conditionals. Find and correct the errors. There may be more than one way to correct some errors.*

The movie industry has changed significantly

since movies were first developed at the beginning

of the twentieth century. By the 1930s, if a film was

made, it belonged to one of the six large studios of

the time. This system worked well because filmmakers

have access to all of the studios' resources from artists

to accountants if they were supported by the large

studios. However, only if the filmmakers agreed to the studios' creative

demands, this arrangement would work. If directors and actors had demanded

more creative control, the studios would release them from their contracts.

Therefore, many filmmakers remained within the studio system and gave

up creative control over their films. While the large studios are still highly influential, other options for filmmaking have emerged since the second half of the twentieth century. Today if a movie is not produced by one of the large studios, it would be called an independent or indie film. Specifically, when a film receives less than half of its funding from a major studio, it was considered an independent film. These films generally have unique content, low budgets, and an uncommon artistic style. Most recently the independent film industry has changed because of inexpensive quality digital film and editing equipment. Whenever someone aspired to be a filmmaker today, it is possible because of this new equipment. If independent filmmakers had not made successful films like *Reservoir Dogs, Little Miss Sunshine*, and *Juno* in the past, aspiring filmmakers today might not have had the fortitude to attempt filmmaking. Another change in the film industry that has helped independent filmmakers is the large number of film festivals. If a filmmaker will want his or her film to be seen, there are thousands of film festivals worldwide every year. A film were to receive a good review at one of these film festivals, the filmmaker may have a career in the ever-changing film industry.

WRITING TOPICS

Most academic essays and research papers require an introduction with a strong thesis statement. The body paragraphs following the introduction support the thesis with references to outside sources. These outside sources might be summarized, quoted, or paraphrased. Notice how the following body paragraph, which was taken from a longer piece of writing, includes a topic sentence, a body with support from outside sources, and a concluding sentence. Use this paragraph as a model when you write about one of the following topics.

Study the use of conditionals in the following student paragraph. Underline each sentence that uses one of the conditional forms that you studied in this chapter.

In the past, it seemed that even if our legislators didn't agree with each other, they still worked together and compromised for the good of the country. This kind of civility has recently been lost. Not only our legislators but the entire country has grown more divided. This growing gap ends progress, for no compromises can be reached on any issue. Many people feel that bipartisan support is essential for achieving progress in the legislature, while others feel it is an impossible goal. For example, former Secretary of State Colin Powell stated on *ABC's Face the Nation*, "It's nice to say let's be bipartisan. But we're a partisan nation. We were raised as a partisan nation."[1] However, if we agree with this, there will be no compromises. The majority party will pass everything without consulting with the minority party or nothing will be passed at all. Both scenarios are unacceptable. Unless something is done to change this hostile environment, both sides will develop such extreme opinions that neither party will be willing to settle. Bipartisanship is important in our society, and, without it, our future looks bleak.

Choose one of the topics below and write at least one paragraph. Find an outside source to support the ideas that you present in your writing. Use several conditional sentences. After you complete your first draft, concentrate on editing your work. Keep in mind the editing practice from this chapter.

1. Write about what you hope or wish for your country or world in the coming years. What has happened in past years to make you wish or hope for this? Write about how your country or the world will be improved if your wish or hope comes true.

2. One of the best ways to learn about ourselves and life is to participate in activities that make us uncomfortable or even scare us. For example, studying in a foreign country, participating in an endurance sport, or making a presentation in front of a large group are activities that are a challenge for some people. What dangerous, adventurous, or new challenge would you like to participate in? Write about why you would attempt this activity and how you would prepare yourself for it. Go on to explain how this would make you a better person in the end.

Go to page 178 for more practice with conditionals.

....

[1] Jake Tapper, Karen Travers, and Huma Khan, "President Obama's Health Care Plan Proposes Fixes to Senate Bill," ABC News/Politics, February 22, 2010, http://abcnews.go.com/ Politics/HealthCare/obama-health-care-plan-fixes-senate-bill-public-option-insurance-reform/ story?id=9908361&page=4.

Sentence Structure and Word Order

GRAMMAR FOCUS

Sentences can have a variety of structures, but all sentences follow rules that determine the order of words within them. Understanding English sentence structure and word order rules will help you use many sentence types correctly and edit for errors such as run-on sentences, sentence fragments, and comma splices.

In the following examples, notice how the same information can be structured in several different ways.

Politicians rarely win elections without large donations from special-interest groups.
Rarely do politicians win elections without large donations from special-interest groups.
Without large donations from special-interest groups, politicians rarely win elections.

Pretest

Check your understanding of sentence structure and word order. Put at check (✓) next to the sentences that are correct.

_____ **1.** To observe the complete rotation of the earth around the sun it takes one year.

_____ **2.** Thoa was educated in Australian and Vietnamese schools; consequently, she speaks English and Vietnamese fluently.

_____ **3.** Because the political science major requires an internship in a government agency.

_____ **4.** The photograph an Ansel Adams original sold for thousands of dollars.

_____ **5.** Istana Nurul Iman is one of the largest homes in the world, it has over 1,700 rooms.

_____ **6.** The final essay will be ten pages long when it is finished.

_____ **7.** After they studied Spanish in Madrid traveled to Italy and France.

_____ **8.** Seldom is the citizenry completely satisfied with the government.

_____ **9.** The researcher questioned does caffeine affect people's sleep habits?

_____ **10.** Approximately 8.7 million people get on the subway in Tokyo every day.

Notice how the sentence structure in the following paragraph gives it an academic tone and makes it interesting to read. Label each of the following underlined grammatical features of this paragraph: a transition word, two prepositional phrases, two clauses, a subject-verb inversion, and a semicolon.

Throughout the world, many awards exist for literary achievement. Some of these awards include the Nobel Prize, the Man Booker Prize, the Miguel de Cervantes Prize, and the Man Asian Literary Prize. One of the most prestigious awards in the United States for newspaper journalism, literature, and musical composition is the Pulitzer Prize. The first Pulitzers were awarded in 1917 after they were established by Joseph A. Pulitzer, who was a journalist and newspaper publisher. Famous recipients of the Pulitzer Prize include President John F. Kennedy, Ernest Hemingway, and Toni Morrison. Seldom is any award without controversy; this is also true of the Pulitzer. Several times in its history, the Pulitzer has been refused by the award winners. However, when the Pulitzer Prizes are announced every April, writers, journalists, and musicians anxiously await the names of the winners.

BASIC SENTENCE ELEMENTS

1. A sentence is a group of words that expresses a complete idea and can stand alone. It must have a subject and a verb. Sentences can be short and simple, but as more information is added to them, they become longer and more complex.

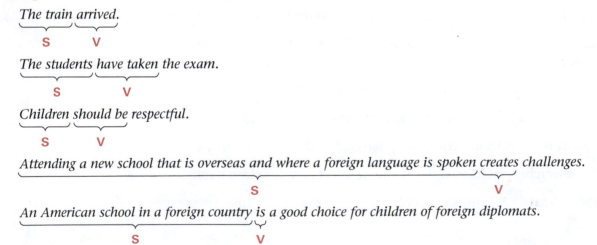

The train arrived.
   S   V

The students have taken the exam.
   S   V

Children should be respectful.
   S   V

Attending a new school that is overseas and where a foreign language is spoken creates challenges.
                               S   V

An American school in a foreign country is a good choice for children of foreign diplomats.
                   S   V

2. Like a sentence, a clause is a group of words with both a subject and a verb. An independent clause can stand alone, while a dependent clause cannot stand alone.

dependent clause   independent clause

When he finished the coursework, he began to work on his Ph.D. dissertation.
     S   V   S   V

not *When finished the coursework, he began to work on his Ph.D. dissertation.*

independent clause   dependent clause

The business received recognition because it uses environmentally sustainable practices.
    S   V   S   V

not *The business received recognition because uses environmentally sustainable practices.*

3. Each sentence can have only one subject; there are several kinds of subjects.

The music assignment *in my music theory class is very difficult.*

not *The music assignment in my music theory class it is very difficult.*

Different kinds of subjects include:

a noun: **Music** *has several subfields at the university.*

a pronoun: **They** *include performance and musicology.*

a noun phrase: **All music majors** *study more than one subfield.*

a gerund phrase: **Studying music** *at the university might include ethnomusicology and music pedagogy.*

an infinitive phrase: **To play** *an instrument well may not be enough to succeed as a music major.*

a noun clause: **Where a student chooses to study music** *depends on the student's area of interest.*

4. Each clause can have only one subject. Do not add a pronoun that repeats the subject within a later clause or part of the sentence.

The **music building** *that is in the middle of campus has many performance studios.*

not *The music building that it is in the middle of campus has many performance studios.*

Mr. and Mrs. Anderson, *who live in Mexico City, do not like the air quality.*

not *Mr. and Mrs. Anderson, who live in Mexico City, they do not like the air quality.*

WRITING TIP

Make sure that all verbs have subjects and that all subjects have verbs. It becomes increasingly important to edit for this point as your sentences become longer and more complex. As you edit, underline the subject and verb of each sentence.

FAULTY SENTENCES

Sentence Fragments

A sentence fragment occurs when one or more of the basic parts of a sentence is missing, generally the subject or the verb.

1. All sentences must have a verb. Without a verb, a sentence is a fragment.

> *Obtaining a Ph.D.* **has been** *her main goal in life.*

> not *Obtaining a Ph.D. her main goal in life.* (sentence fragment)

2. A dependent clause contains a subject and a verb, but it does not express a complete idea and cannot stand alone. Dependent clauses can begin with subordinating conjunctions such as *if, unless, before, after, when, while, since, because,* or *although.* A dependent clause must be joined to an independent or main clause in order to form a complete sentence. A dependent clause that stands alone is a sentence fragment, not a complete sentence.

> **Because the water supply has decreased**, *the city is rationing water.*

> not *Because the water supply has decreased.* (sentence fragment)

3. A phrase that stands alone is also a sentence fragment because it does not have a subject and a verb. A phrase must be joined to an independent clause or have a subject and a verb added to it in order to form a complete sentence.

> *Many architects go to Italy* **to study the architecture of the Renaissance period.**

> not *To study the architecture of the Renaissance period.* (fragment/infinitive phrase)

> *The Renaissance cathedral is* **next to the building on the corner**.

> not *Next to the building on the corner.* (sentence fragment/prepositional phrase)

WRITING TIP

The number of words or the length of a phrase or clause does not tell you if it is a complete sentence or not. *Attending a new school that is overseas and where a foreign language is spoken* contains many words, but it is a phrase, not a sentence. A sentence must contain a main verb: *Attending a new school that is overseas and where a foreign language is spoken* **can be** *an exciting experience.*

Run-on Sentences

A run-on sentence occurs when two complete sentences are placed together without any punctuation between them.

A period or a semicolon must be used at the end of a sentence before the next sentence begins to avoid a run-on sentence. A semicolon is similar to a period, but it is generally used to separate two closely related sentences.

> *Good writers use the writing process**;** they write, revise, and edit repeatedly.*

> not *Good writers use the writing process they write, revise, and edit repeatedly.* (run-on sentence)

Comma Splices

A comma splice occurs when two complete sentences are separated by a comma.

A period or a semicolon, not a comma, must be used at the end of a sentence to avoid a comma splice. Use a semicolon when the information in the two clauses is closely related.

> *American football is a dangerous sport. The injury rate seems to increase annually.*

> not *American football is a dangerous sport, the injury rate seems to increase annually.* (comma splice)

Self Check 1

Circle the sentence that uses sentence structure correctly.

1. **(a)** Working on the computer over long periods of time.

   (b) Working on the computer over long periods of time results in eye strain.

2. **(a)** The bus is always late; commuters can never rely on it.

   (b) The bus is always late commuters can never rely on it.

3. **(a)** Professor Marin usually early to class.

   (b) Professor Marin is usually early to class.

4. **(a)** Public speaking for many people it causes anxiety.

   (b) Public speaking for many people causes anxiety.

5. **(a)** White wedding dresses that they symbolize purity appeared during the Victorian era.

   (b) White wedding dresses that symbolize purity appeared during the Victorian era.

USING SENTENCE STRUCTURE

Making Writing Interesting

1. Add details to an independent clause at its beginning, middle, or end to make sentences longer, more complex, and more interesting to read. See the following examples for the sentence:

   The assignment is time consuming.

   • at the beginning:

   Requiring hours of work, *the assignment is time consuming.*

   Due to its numerous experiments, *the assignment is time consuming.*

   Because it requires numerous experiments, *the assignment is time consuming.*

- in the middle:

The assignment **for English 101A** *is time consuming.*

The assignment, **a 25-page paper,** *is time consuming.*

The assignment **that is required before graduation** *is time consuming.*

- at the end:

The assignment is time consuming, **allowing me only three hours of sleep per night**.

The assignment is time consuming **due to its numerous experiments.**

The assignment is time consuming **although it is also very interesting**.

2. Vary the sentence structure within a paragraph or essay. Begin sentences with a clause, phrase, or conjunction rather than always starting with the subject. This will make your writing more interesting to read.

Beginning with a clause:

Because the birth rate is declining in Korea, *the Korean government has provided tax incentives to families with two or more children.*

Beginning with a phrase:

In the Czech Republic, Ukraine, and Poland, *birth rates are among the lowest in the world.*

Beginning with a conjunction or transition:

Birth rates are declining in many developed countries. **Yet,** *the worldwide birth rate continues to rise.* **Consequently,** *the environment and global food supplies are in jeopardy.*

3. Use coordinating conjunctions, subordinating conjunctions, or transitions to develop relationships within and between sentences.

- to expand on ideas within or between sentences use:

Coordinating conjunctions: *and*

Economics teaches us that when supply goes up, demand goes down, **and** *when supply goes down, demand goes up.*

Transitions: *additionally, also, furthermore, in addition, moreover*

Economics is used to understand business, finance, and government. **In addition,** *crime, education, and health are studied from an economic perspective.*

- to contrast ideas within or between sentences use:

Coordinating conjunctions: *but, yet*

Many people attempt to learn a second language, **but** *only a few are successful.*

Transitions: *however, in contrast, nevertheless, on the other hand*

Translating is not an effective way to learn a new language. **However,** *many students rely on it.*

Subordinating conjunctions: *although, even though, though, whereas, while*

Most people in Europe speak two or three languages **whereas** *most people in the United States speak only one.*

- to show alternatives within or between sentences use:

Coordinating conjunctions: *or*

The use of fossil fuel must be reduced **or** *life on earth will change dramatically.*

Transitions: *instead, otherwise*

> *Clean forms of energy are necessary;* **otherwise,** *pollution will continue to rise.*

Subordinating conjunctions: *unless*

> **Unless** *all people in the world help reduce pollution, everyone will be negatively affected.*

NOTE: The subordinating conjunction *unless* generally means *if . . . not*.

> **If** *all people in the world do* **not** *help reduce pollution, everyone will be negatively affected.*

- to show results within or between sentences use:

Coordinating conjunctions: *for, so*

> *Some students attend school overseas,* **so** *they learn a new language naturally.*

Transitions: *as a result, consequently, therefore, thus*

> *Many language learners immerse themselves in the new language and culture;* **as a result,** *they learn the new language quickly.*

Subordinating conjunctions: *as, because, since, so . . . that, such . . . that*

> *Many people in the United States choose to study Spanish* **because** *Mexico is an important neighbor.*

WRITING TIP

Good writers vary the length of their sentences within a piece of writing. A short sentence of three to four words can be very effective if it is used after several longer sentences. To create interesting, complicated sentences, begin with a simple sentence and slowly add more words, phrases, and clauses until it clearly conveys your meaning. Use the rules in this section to add details to your sentences one step at a time, but remember to use a combination of short and long sentences within a piece of writing.

Using Punctuation Correctly

1. A period ends affirmative and negative statements, indirect questions, and commands.

> *A lunar calendar shows the phases of the moon. It does not show lunar eclipses.*

> *The investigator asked the suspect where he was at the time of the crime.*

> *Finish the work by 10:00 tonight.*

2. A question mark ends a direct question.

> *Where is the support of the thesis statement?*

> NOT *Many students wonder where they should place the support of the thesis statement?*

3. An exclamation point ends a statement with emphasis.

> *Watch out!*

4. Commas appear in several different locations.

- Commas separate items in a list.

> *Essays will be graded on* **content, organization, grammar,** *and* **mechanics.**

- Commas appear after an independent clause before a coordinating conjunction.

  Applicants must have good writing skills, but *they must also possess good oral communication skills.*

- Commas appear after a phrase or clause before an independent clause.

  Over the past three years, *the company's expenses have been greater than its profits.*

  If this occurs again, *the company may declare bankruptcy.*

- Commas appear after transition words.

  Exercising outside on hot days places stress on the body. **However,** *drinking plenty of fluids helps prevent some of the health risks.*

5. A semicolon separates two sentences with closely related information and two sentences with a transition.

  *Many volunteer positions are available in the United States and abroad**;** professionals can find meaningful volunteer work in a variety of fields.*

  *Volunteer work looks impressive on work and academic applications**; moreover,** it can be emotionally rewarding.*

Notice that a comma follows the transitional word.

6. A colon adds further explanation at the end of a sentence. A single word, a phrase, a sentence, or a list can follow the colon.

  *Healthy aging depends on a variety of factors**: physical, social, mental, and financial**.*

7. Dashes separate words from the rest of a sentence and call attention to them.

  The Tang Dynasty—one of the longest Chinese dynasties—lasted for 289 years.

Self Check 2

Circle the sentence that uses sentence structure correctly.

1. (a) The executive position, which it is vice president of marketing, pays over $100,000 per year.

 (b) The executive position, vice president of marketing, pays over $100,000 per year.

2. (a) A sunburn can cause blisters, chills, and fever in addition it can lead to skin cancer.

 (b) A sunburn can cause blisters, chills, and fever. In addition, it can lead to skin cancer.

3. (a) Swimming is allowed in the ocean unless the bacteria level is too high.

 (b) Swimming is not allowed in the ocean unless the bacteria level is too high.

4. (a) A funeral is a ceremony that is practiced throughout the world to mark a person's death, however, the ceremonies vary among cultures.

 (b) A funeral is a ceremony that is practiced throughout the world to mark a person's death; however, the ceremonies vary among cultures.

5. (a) Many factors comprise the final course grade: participation, homework, essays, and exams.

(b) Many factors comprise the final course grade. Participation, homework, essays, and exams.

WORD ORDER RULES

In addition to the basic sentence structure rules that you've been studying, there are a few word order rules that are important to follow if a sentence is to be constructed correctly.

Basic Word Order

1. Word order in English sentences must follow one of two patterns: (a) subject + verb + object or (b) subject + verb + complement. An object is a noun, pronoun, or noun phrase that follows a transitive verb and takes the action of that verb. A complement is generally an adjective or a noun that follows a nonaction verb and describes the subject.

(a) *The students are studying a formula.*
      S   V   O

(b) *The students are diligent.*
      S   V   C

This basic word order must remain the same as additional information is added to the basic sentence.

In the math lab, the diligent students who have a quiz tomorrow are studying
                  S   V

several new formulas.
      O

2. Many transitive verbs are followed by an object. The object receives the action of the verb. An object can also show to whom or for whom an action occurs. When a sentence contains two objects, the word order generally follows one of two patterns.

SUBJECT + VERB	TO/FOR WHOM OR WHAT DOES THE ACTION OCCUR?	WHO OR WHAT IS RECEIVING THE ACTION?	TO/FOR WHOM OR WHAT DOES THE ACTION OCCUR?
(a) The president gave	a soldier	the medal of honor.	
(b) The president gave		the medal of honor	to a soldier.

NOTE: In pattern (b), most verbs use the preposition *to;* however, some use the preposition *for.*

Verbs that use the preposition *to* include:

bring	mail	sell	teach
give	offer	send	tell
hand	pass	serve	throw
lend	read	show	toss

Verbs that use the preposition *for* include:

build	cook	leave	order
buy	find	make	save

Verbs that use both prepositions *to* and *for* include:

do	pay	take
get	sing	write

WRITING TIP

Do not translate word order or sentence structure from your native language. Consider analyzing your native language and noticing how it differs from English to understand some of the word order errors you may make in English.

3. Use statement word order (subject + verb) in sentences with indirect questions. Indirect questions are noun clauses that are considered statements, not questions.

> *Alexi wonders* **when <u>the full moon</u> <u>occurs</u>.**

> not *Alexi wonders when does the full moon occur?*

> *Do you know* **where <u>the financial aid office</u> <u>is?</u>**

> not *Do you know where is the financial aid office?*

NOTE: *If* can be used for indirect questions that answer *yes/no* questions.

> *Does a rattlesnake bite result in death?*

> *The children asked* **if a rattlesnake bite results in death**.

4. Use inverted word order (verb + subject) when placing negative adverbs such as *seldom, never, rarely, only once,* or *not only* at the beginning of a sentence.

> **Never <u>has</u> <u>the food industry</u>** *produced cheaper food.*

> not *Never the food industry has produced cheaper food.*

> **Not only <u>has</u> <u>the food industry</u>** *produced cheaper food, but it is supplying more of it.*

> not *Not only the food industry has produced cheaper food, but it is supplying more of it.*

5. Use inverted word order when a prepositional phrase begins a sentence that has an intransitive verb (a verb that cannot take an object). This form is usually used to describe a location.

> **On the floor <u>lie</u> <u>two beautiful Persian rugs</u>.**

> **Down the road <u>strolled</u> <u>two men</u>.**

> **In the corner <u>is</u> <u>an old rocking chair</u>.**

> not *In the corner an old rocking chair is.*

Word Order with Phrasal Verbs

Verbs such as *hand in, call back,* and *pick up* are called phrasal verbs or two-word verbs. These verbs consist of a verb and one or more particles. Particles look like prepositions, but they change the meaning of the verb. Phrasal verbs are either separable or nonseparable.

- Separable phrasal verbs:

    An unhappy employee **handed in** *his resignation.*

    An unhappy employee **handed** *his resignation* **in**.

With separable phrasal verbs, a noun can come after the phrasal verb or between the verb and the particle. A pronoun must always come between the verb and the particle.

    Dr. Finder **picked up** *the package.*

    Dr. Finder **picked** *the package* **up**.

    Dr. Finder **picked <u>it</u> up**.

    not *Dr. Finder picked up it.*

Some separable phrasal verbs include:

ask out	find out	pick up	tear down
call back	give back	put away	tear off
call off	give up	put back	tear up
call up	hand in	put down	throw away/out
cross out	hand out	put off	try on
do over	hang up	put on	turn down
figure out	leave out	put out	turn off
fill in	look up	shut off	turn on
fill out	make up	start over	turn up
fill up	pay back	take off	write down

- Nonseparable phrasal verbs:

    The car **ran into** *the light post.*

    not *The car ran the light post into.*

    not *The car ran it into.*

Some nonseparable phrasal verbs include:

call on	get off	keep on
drop in	get on	look out (for)
drop out (of)	get out (of)	run into
get along (with)	get over	run out (of)
get back (from)	get through (with)	watch out (for)
get in(to)	grow up	

Word Order with Noun Modifiers

Adjectives

Single-word adjectives come before the nouns they describe. If more than one adjective describes a noun, there is generally a fixed order in which the adjectives appear. A noun usually has no more than a determiner and three adjectives describing it.

DETERMINER	NUMBER	OPINION	PHYSICAL DESCRIPTION	ORIGIN	MATERIAL	NOUN MODIFIER	NOUN
a		precious	round	South African			diamond
	three		large			hunting	dogs
some		beautiful	green		wooden		chairs

> A **precious round South African diamond** *was found in 1952.*
>
> **Three large hunting dogs** *didn't catch the fox that they were chasing.*
>
> *The store has* **some beautiful green wooden chairs**.

NOTES:

1. If two or more adjectives fall within the same category, they are separated by a comma. These adjectives can also be reversed or separated by *and* or *or*.

   Good teachers should be **creative, well rounded, <u>and</u> knowledgeable.**

2. When two or more adjectives fall within separate categories and make sense in only one order, no commas are needed.

   Three heavy wool *sweaters arrived in the mail yesterday.*

Prepositional Phrases

Prepositional phrases that modify nouns generally follow the nouns.

> *Work* **at nuclear power plants** *has dangerous aspects.*
>
> not *Work has dangerous aspects at nuclear power plants.*

Adjective Clauses

Adjective clauses closely follow the nouns that they describe or modify.

> *The entrance exam* **that new students took** *was given the first day of class.*
>
> not *The entrance exam was given the first day of class that new students took.*

Word Order with Adverbs

1. Adverbs may appear at the beginning, middle, or end of sentences depending on the type of adverb. There are adverbs of time, manner, frequency, and place. There are also adverbs that comment on what has been said.

   Although the order of adverbs and adverb phrases within a sentence can vary, the following guidelines can be helpful.

- Initial position

Time:	**Last night/Yesterday/Two days ago** *there was a wildfire in Montana.*
Opinion:	**Clearly/Honestly/Of course**, *the ticket price is too high.*
Manner:	**Quickly/Happily/Carefully**, *the players ran down the soccer field.*

- Middle position

Frequency:	*Business executives* **always/never/seldom** *go on a vacation.*
	They are **often/usually/constantly** *at work.*
Manner:	*The teacher* **softly/enthusiastically/sadly** *announced our grades.*

- End position

Place:	*The children play* **outside/in the park/here**.
Time:	*They begin volunteering* **next week/tomorrow/in one month**.
Manner:	*The doubles tennis team played that ball* **well/poorly/badly**.

NOTE: No more than two or three adverbials generally appear in one sentence.

> **Every year,** *some families* **happily** *return* **to the same vacation spot.**

Adverbs of time and frequency usually come after those of position and direction.

> *The orchestra played* **in the new concert hall** <u>last night</u>.

> *Students, faculty, and staff drive* **to school** <u>every Monday</u> *because parking is free.*

WRITING TIP

Formal academic writing generally places adverbs in the middle position. Follow the guidelines given in the explanation above, but whenever possible, place adverbs in the middle position.

Less formal:	*The lottery winners have not been contacted yet.*
More formal:	*The lottery winners have not yet been contacted.*
Less academic:	*Generally, foreign languages are found in the Humanities Department.*
More academic:	*Foreign languages are generally found in the Humanities Department.*

2. Adverbs should be as close as possible to the verbs, adjectives, adverbs, or clauses that they modify.

> *Mara works* **diligently** *in the lab.* (*Diligently* modifies the verb *works*.)

> *Tivoli Gardens in Denmark is* **very** *beautiful.* (*Very* modifies the adjective *beautiful*.)

> *It is possible to learn sign language* **surprisingly** *quickly.* (*Surprisingly* modifies the adverb *quickly*.)

> **Amazingly,** *the plane arrived on time.* (*Amazingly* modifies the entire clause.)

3. Adverbs such as *a lot*, *a little*, and *slightly* limit the word they modify and appear before that word.

> *Ms. Kelly is* **tired** *today.*

> *Ms. Kelly is* <u>**a lot**</u> **more tired** *today than she was yesterday.*

> *Ms. Kelly is* <u>**a little**</u> **more tired** *today than she was yesterday.*

> *Ms. Kelly is* <u>**slightly**</u> **more tired** *today than she was yesterday.*

4. The adverb *only* may appear in several locations within a sentence. Its position changes the meaning of the sentence.

> Dieters **only** *weigh themselves once a week.* (The one thing dieters do once a week is weigh themselves.)

> **Only** *dieters weigh themselves once a week.* (Dieters are the only people who weigh themselves once a week.)

> *Dieters weigh themselves* **only** *once a week.* (Dieters do not weigh themselves more than once a week.)

Self Check 3

Circle the sentence that uses word order correctly.

1. (a) The carbon-fiber German racing cars are winning the Formula One events.

   (b) The German carbon-fiber racing cars are winning the Formula One events.

2. (a) The judge called the attorney on to answer the question.

   (b) The judge called on the attorney to answer the question.

3. (a) Italian ice cream is especially good.

   (b) Especially, Italian ice cream is good.

4. (a) The librarian is reading to the class the school's plagiarism policy.

   (b) The librarian is reading the school's plagiarism policy to the class.

5. (a) Not only she received an award for writing, but she is also being considered for other awards.

   (b) Not only did she receive an award for writing, but she is also being considered for other awards.

EDITING PRACTICE

1. *Put a check (✓) next to the sentences that use sentence structure and word order correctly. Correct the sentences that have errors.*

_____ **1.** School begins in three days, therefore, students need to buy their school supplies soon.

_____ **2.** Developers must follow strict building standards; otherwise, they face large fines.

_____ **3.** Several years ago in Iceland there was a big earthquake, hundreds of people were killed.

_____ **4.** Protecting the environment—air, water, and land—is the world's biggest challenge.

_____ **5.** Downloading music without paying for it is illegal. Furthermore, it harms the music industry as well as the artists who compose and perform the music.

_____ **6.** While herbal supplements are promoted by many people others are not convinced of their benefits.

_____ **7.** On the Fourth of July, Americans celebrate the independence of the United States.

_____ **8.** Eyesight diminishes with age, it is the only health decline that happens to all people.

_____ **9.** Most petroleum from the Canadian large oil fields is exported to the United States.

_____ **10.** By reading the user manual for the new phone.

_____ **11.** The chemistry class is full many students are trying to register for it.

_____ **12.** When they finished the class project, their summer vacation began.

_____ **13.** At the end of the introductory paragraphs belongs the thesis statement.

_____ **14.** It is not clear why did the nuclear industry lose support?

_____ **15.** The health care industry is facing a crisis because has insufficient doctors and nurses to fill its needs.

_____ **16.** Travelers who cross several time zones by plane they experience jet lag.

2. _In the following paragraph, the underlined words, phrases, or clauses have sentence structure or word order errors. Write your corrections above each error. There may be more than one way to correct some errors._

(1) <u>Some people have wondered does technology make their life easier or not.</u> (2) <u>This may be answered when one thinks of household conveniences the dishwasher, vacuum cleaner, washing machine, and garbage disposal.</u> Of course, life is easier with these important inventions. However, have more recent innovations such as the Internet, computer, and mobile phone improved our lives? (3) <u>Life is certainly more convenient we do not have to hunt for a pay phone, go to the library, or drive to the mall or grocery store anymore.</u> (4) <u>Almost everything that we need to know or purchase it can be found at the click of a mouse or tap of the finger.</u> No one would deny that technology brings time-saving advantages. However, it also brings

disadvantages. (5) <u>Some people miss the "good old days" because could escape work at the end of the day.</u> (6) <u>Rarely today's workers are able to get away from their workplace because of the constant access to their attention and time that mobile phones and computers provide.</u> (7) <u>The good news is that people have the ultimate control, they can turn off these devices.</u> It seems that technology has made life easier as long as we control it and do not let it control us.

3. *All punctuation and capitalization have been left out of the following paragraph. Using what you know about sentence structure and word order, replace the punctuation and capitalization.*

we admire the honesty of abraham lincoln and george washington and according to thomas jefferson "honesty is the first chapter of the book of wisdom" yet lessons about telling the truth are some of the most difficult for humans to follow it seems that the most intelligent animals are the most likely to lie we might then ask ourselves if humans are destined to lie research shows that most children lie nearly every hour students tell two lies per day and the average adult lies once a day this behavior may be due to our inability to detect lies humans are able to identify a lie only about 50 percent of the time while some lies are malicious the majority are told out of kindness you look good today I love your dress and this tastes delicious these are the kinds of lies that hold society together according to some experts although society says that it values truth it may be the lies that keep us together

4. *The following paragraph has ten sentence structure or word order errors. Find and correct the errors.*

During the nineteenth century, many groups of people tried to form utopian communities, one of the most famous was called Brook Farm. Which was located in the state of Massachusetts. Like many utopian communities,

Brook Farm was based on religious principles, and its main goal was to treat all people equally. Many members of utopian communities thought that the Industrial Revolution of the mid-nineteenth century it had caused people to suffer and made work undignified. Therefore, they

established communities where people received fair wages and equal status for all types of work. With no difference between physical and mental work. All utopians were idealists they wanted to end the separation and differences between people. Was a noble goal, but most of the utopian communities were ultimately unsuccessful for a number of different reasons social, economic, administrative, and religious. This failure did not stop more modern utopian communities that they were founded during the Vietnam era of the 1960s from pursuing their dream of living in a peaceful world. Because of the U.S. involvement in Vietnam during this time, many wondered how could they promote a nonviolent world. Unfortunately, human nature doomed these communities to failure. Seldom people have been able to live by placing communal goals over personal goals.

WRITING TOPICS

Most academic essays and research papers require an introduction with a strong thesis statement. The body paragraphs that follow the introduction support the thesis with references to outside sources. These outside sources might be summarized, quoted, or paraphrased. Notice how the following body paragraph, which was taken from a longer piece of writing, includes a topic sentence, a body with support from outside sources, and a concluding sentence. Use this paragraph as a model when you write about one of the following topics.

Study the sentence structure and word order in the following student paragraph. Locate and underline examples of the kinds of sentence structure and word order rules that you studied in this chapter.

Of the four stages of the writing process, the prewriting stage may be the most important. According to the Purdue Online Writing Lab, "Writing is a process, not merely a product,"[1] and this process begins with prewriting. Some of the elements to consider during the prewriting stage are the topic, the audience, and the assignment's purpose. Once these have been clarified by brainstorming, which includes talking, reading, and free writing about the topic, a writer should have developed a working thesis. At this point, the experts at the Purdue Online Writing Lab suggest to "just start writing."[2] Grammar, format, punctuation, and spelling are not important at this stage in the writing process. The point of prewriting is to get all ideas down on paper so that they can be evaluated at a later point. Having all his or her ideas on paper, the writer can now cut out, add, and elaborate on them. To organize these ideas, some writers use a basic outline structure, while others list or cluster their ideas into logical patterns. Although all stages of the writing process are important and necessary, rarely do students devote enough time to the prewriting stage. By taking time to think thoroughly about the topic at the beginning of the writing process, students will save time during later stages and finish with a better developed and organized essay.

Choose one of the topics below and write at least one paragraph. Find an outside source to support the ideas that you present in your writing. Practice using the different types of sentence structure and word order that you have studied. After you complete your first draft, concentrate on editing your work. Keep in mind the editing practice from this chapter.

1. Describe the writing process. Think about the different stages of the writing process: prewriting, writing, revising, and editing. Write a description that includes all steps within the process or focuses more deeply on one of the steps.

2. Fear is a universal emotion that everyone has experienced at some point in life. Some common fears are the fear of flying, public speaking, or heights. Explain how people can overcome fear. Write about one particular kind of fear and techniques to overcome it or techniques that might work for several different types of fear.

Go to pages 178 and 180 for more practice with sentence structure and word order.

....

[1] "Invention: Starting the Writing Process," OWL Purdue Online Writing Lab, accessed July 14, 2011, http://owl.english.purdue.edu/owl/resource/587/01/.

[2] "Invention."

Noun Clauses and Using Sources

GRAMMAR FOCUS

Noun clauses are used in the same way as nouns and have a subject and verb like all clauses. Noun clauses are also used in reported or indirect speech to express a person's thoughts or ideas. Indirect speech as well as quoted or direct speech is necessary in academic writing to support the ideas or argument in a paper. This chapter provides practice with noun clauses and direct and indirect speech as well as using outside sources to strengthen your writing. Notice how the following sentences express the same information through direct speech, indirect speech, and a noun clause.

DIRECT SPEECH	On the first day of class, the professor stated, "All the information from my lectures will be on the exams."
INDIRECT SPEECH	On the first day of class, the professor said that all the information from his lecture would be on the exams.
NOUN CLAUSE	What the professor announced on the first day of class was that all the information from his lectures would be on the exams.

Pretest

Check your understanding of noun clauses, direct speech, and indirect speech. Put a check (✓) next to the sentences that are correct.

_____ **1.** The judge informed the jury that the defendant had chosen to be his own lawyer.

_____ **2.** Why elderly people begin to lose their short-term memories are an important area of research.

_____ **3.** Whales spend the winter in the warm waters of Mexico has created a tourist industry there.

_____ **4.** Cardiologist Lakshmi Singh remarked, "Although patients may not want to take medication, it is necessary when arteries have built up too much plaque."

_____ **5.** The reporter asked the athlete when is he going to retire?

_____ **6.** Most cities demand the public be required to recycle garbage.

_____ **7.** A nutritionist recommended me to eat more fruits and vegetables.

_____ **8.** The oil companies announced that unrest in the region would result in higher gas prices.

_____ **9.** Because of the country's political instability, the ambassador warns, "We must end the political unrest before we can discuss the rising cost of imports."

_____ **10.** The science teacher taught the children that water froze at 32° F.

Notice how the following paragraph uses a noun clause, direct speech, and indirect speech. Underline one example of each of these.

When we are stressed, we are often unable to make good decisions. Excessive stress can also have negative effects on our organs and tissues. It additionally tends to control us emotionally, as we become angry, fearful, and even depressed. Stress may impair spiritual development as well. We may no longer see our purpose, for we are focused on the immediate cause of our stress rather than long-term goals. What these symptoms tell us about stress is that it has the ability to cause long-term damage to our bodies. To prevent permanent damage, we must learn coping and relaxation skills to manage stress. One of the best ways of accomplishing this is through meditation. By quieting the mind, we release stress and regain control. It allows us to redirect our focus from the problem to the solution. Dr. Melissa Conrad Stöppler, an assistant professor of pathology at Georgetown University, states that one of the best ways to reduce stress is through exercise. "Exercise can emotionally remove one temporarily from a stressful environment or situation," she says. "Being fit and healthy also increases one's ability to deal with stress as it arises."

FORMING NOUN CLAUSES

1. A noun clause is a clause that functions in the same way as a noun. A noun clause begins with either *that*, *if*, or a *wh-* word and can appear at the beginning, in the middle, or at the end of a sentence.

that	**That the weather was bad** *caused the late delivery.*
	The reason [that] the delivery arrived late *was the snowstorm in Toronto.*
	The pilots knew **[that] the weather was dangerous for landing**, *so the delivery arrived late.*
what	**What draws people to reality television** *is the conflicts among cast members.*
when	*The Secretary of the Treasury doesn't know* **when the economic crisis will end**, *which causes uncertainty in the global markets.*
where	**Where crimes will occur** *is difficult to predict.*
why	*It is clear* **why manufacturing jobs are moving overseas.**
how	*The economist explained* **how inflation grew during the past decade.**
whether/if	*The military doesn't know* **whether it will be able to recruit enough soldiers** *because of the sacrifices required of enlisted men and women.*

NOTE: *Whether or not* or *if* can be used for sentences that answer indirect yes/no questions.

> *The government is not sure **if** electric cars are the solution to our dependence on oil.*

> *The government is not certain **whether or not** alternative forms of energy will reduce our dependence on oil.*

or

> *The government is questioning **whether** nuclear energy is safe **or not**.*

2. *That* can be omitted at the beginning of a noun clause if the noun clause is the object or complement of the sentence. Note: A complement follows the verb *be* and other nonaction verbs such as *seem, look,* and *appear.*

> *Cab drivers think* **[that] their profession is one of the most stressful.**

> *Studies show* **[that] there are many cab drivers with stress-related illnesses.**

The word *that* cannot be omitted when the noun clause is the subject of the sentence.

> **That driving a cab is dangerous** *makes it difficult to find drivers.*

> not *Driving a cab is dangerous makes it difficult to find drivers.*

Frequently *it* functions as the subject of a sentence and is followed by *be* + adjective. The noun clause, a complement, occurs at the end of the sentence. *That* can be omitted, but it is generally included in formal writing.

> **It** *appears* **[that] driving a cab is a very stressful profession.**

3. When a noun clause is the subject of a sentence, use the third-person singular verb.

> **How the prisoners escaped <u>is</u>** *under investigation.*

> **That the prison's security systems failed <u>was</u>** *a major factor in the escape.*

4. Noun clauses use statement word order (subject + verb), not question word order (verb + subject). Neither the auxiliaries *do, does, did,* and *be* nor question marks are used in noun clauses.

> *The government wonders where the instigators of the political unrest are.*

S   V

> not *The government wonders where are the instigators of the political unrest?*

> *Why the political unrest began is evident to outsiders.*

S   V

> not *Why did the political unrest begin is evident to outsiders?*

5. Use the base form of the verb after adjectives or verbs of urgency or request. The base form of the verb is also used with third-person singular subjects (*he, she,* and *it*). For these kinds of noun clauses that are negative, use *not* without an auxiliary verb.

Adjectives of urgency: *critical, crucial, desirable, essential, imperative, important, necessary, urgent, vital*

> *It was* **essential** *[that] the diplomats* **attend** *the meeting.*

adjective of urgency   subject   base verb

> *It is* **important** *that he* **not arrive** *late.*

Adjectives of request: *best, recommended*

It is **best** for the patient [that] the medicine **be** taken every two hours.

> adjective of request   subject base
>   verb

It is **recommended** [that] one **not take** the advanced course before the introductory course.

Verbs of urgency: *command, demand, insist, order, urge*

Most parents **insist** [that] their child **be** home by curfew.

> verb of urgency   subject base
>   verb

The police **urged** [that] minors **not return** home after curfew.

Verbs of request or suggestion: *advise, ask, prefer, propose, recommend, request, suggest*

My counselor **is proposing** [that] I **not take** the course for a grade.

> verb of suggestion   subject base
>   verb

WRITING TIP

Always choose formal language rather than informal when writing for academic purposes. A noun clause is considered more formal than an infinitive phrase.

Less formal: *It is necessary for us to complete the research by the end of the week.*

More formal: *It is necessary that we complete the research by the end of the week.*

USING NOUN CLAUSES

Noun clauses commonly follow a number of verbs, adjectives, and expressions.

Verbs

agree	fear	learn	recognize
assume	feel	notice	regret
believe	figure out	observe	remember
care	find out	predict	reveal
conclude	forget	presume	show
decide	hear	pretend	suppose
demonstrate	hope	prove	suspect
discover	imagine	read	teach
doubt	indicate	realize	think
dream	know	recall	understand

Research **indicates** [that] **the current medical treatment will not change.**

The travelers **suspect** [that] **the flight may be postponed.**

Adjectives

afraid	disappointed/disappointing	proud
amazed/amazing	fortunate	shocked/shocking
angry	furious	sorry
ashamed	happy	sure
astounded/astounding	horrified/horrifying	surprised/surprising
aware	impossible	strange
certain	lucky	terrified/terrifying
clear	obvious	thrilled/thrilling
convinced/convincing	pleased/pleasing	true
delighted/delightful	positive	worried

University admissions officers are **shocked** **[that] student enrollment has declined.**

It is **fortunate** **[that] the results support the earlier conclusion.**

Expressions

the effect that	the possibility that
the fact that	the reason that
the idea that	the way that

The idea [that] some languages are harder to learn than others *is a myth.*

The possibility [that] the senator will be reelected *is small.*

Self Check 1

Circle the sentence that forms or uses the noun clause correctly.

1. **(a)** The chemist is wondering where the molecular compounds are.

   (b) The chemist is wondering where are the molecular compounds?

2. **(a)** How quickly the cells divide depend on the health of the cells.

   (b) How quickly the cells divide depends on the health of the cells.

3. **(a)** When Australians typically celebrate is with picnics or barbecues.

   (b) How Australians typically celebrate is with picnics or barbecues.

4. **(a)** That exercise reduces blood pressure is commonly accepted.

   (b) Exercise reduces blood pressure is commonly accepted.

5. **(a)** It is desirable that a foreign-language student use a dictionary in the new language rather than a translating dictionary.

   (b) It is desirable that a foreign-language student uses a dictionary in the new language rather than a translating dictionary.

USING NOUN CLAUSES IN INDIRECT SPEECH

1. Indirect or reported speech occurs when you report your own or someone else's thoughts, ideas, or words. Indirect speech requires the use of noun clauses.

   I told the producer **[that] her films had always been my favorite.**

   Professor Mahini said **[that] many of her students do volunteer work in the community**.

   We asked the global positioning system **where the nearest gas station was**.

2. The verb tense changes when a quotation is changed to indirect speech.

DIRECT SPEECH/QUOTATION	INDIRECT SPEECH	COMMENTS
Hillary Rodham Clinton said, "I **have worked** persistently on issues relating to women, children, and families . . . I **want** to speak for mothers who **are fighting** for good schools, safe neighborhoods, clean air, and clean airwaves."	Hillary Rodham Clinton said [that] she **had worked** persistently on issues relating to women, children, and families . . . [that] she **wanted** to speak for mothers who **were fighting** for good schools, safe neighborhoods, clean air, and clean airwaves.	When the verb in the quotation is in the present time, it generally changes to the past time in indirect speech. simple present → simple past present progressive → past progressive present perfect → past perfect
While speaking about the Vietnam War in 1967, Martin Luther King, Jr. said, "We **were taking** the black young men who **were crippled** by our society and sending them 8,000 miles away to guarantee liberties in Southeast Asia which they **had not found** in southwest Georgia and East Harlem."	While speaking about the Vietnam War in 1967, Martin Luther King, Jr. said [that] they **had been taking** the black young men who **had been crippled** by their society and sending them 8,000 miles away to guarantee liberties in Southeast Asia which they **had not found** in southwest Georgia and East Harlem.	When the verb in the quotation is in the past time, it generally changes to one of the past perfect forms in indirect speech. simple past → past perfect past progressive → past perfect progressive past perfect → past perfect
At a graduation ceremony, former First Lady Barbara Pierce Bush said, "You **are never going to regret** not having passed one more test, winning one more verdict, or not closing one more deal. You **will regret** time not spent with a husband, a child, a friend, or a parent."	At a graduation ceremony, former First Lady Barbara Pierce Bush said [that] you **were never going to regret** not having passed one more test, winning one more verdict, or not closing one more deal. You **would regret** time not spent with a husband, a child, a friend, or a parent.	When the verb in the quotation is in the future time, the verb form changes in indirect speech. *will* → *would* *be going to* → *was/were going to*

3. Some modals change when direct speech changes to indirect speech.

MODAL	DIRECT SPEECH	INDIRECT SPEECH
can → *could*	The CEO announced, "We **can** reduce the company's debt."	The CEO announced [that] they **could** reduce the company's debt.
may → *might*	She said, "It **may** take a few years to reduce the debt completely."	She said [that] it **might** take a few years to reduce the debt completely.
has to → *had to*	She said, "The finance team **has to** study the sales projections."	She said that the finance team **had to** study the sales projections.
must → *had to*	She said, "All employees **must** reduce expenses."	She said that all employees **had to** reduce expenses.

4. Other modals do not change when direct speech changes to indirect speech.

MODAL	DIRECT SPEECH	INDIRECT SPEECH
should	The leader of the study group said, "We **should** study at the coffee house."	The leader of the study group said [that] they **should** study at the coffee house.
could	He said, "She **could** use the wireless there."	He said [that] she **could** use the wireless there.
might	He said, "It **might** be quieter at the library."	He said [that] it **might** be quieter at the library.
could have	He said, "She **could have** brought her laptop."	He said [that] she **could have** brought her laptop.
should have	He said, "They **should have** studied more."	He said [that] they **should have** studied more.

5. Indirect speech may remain in the present if the statement is still true, is a fact, or was recently reported.

DIRECT SPEECH	INDIRECT SPEECH
Barack Obama said, "My father's family **comes** from Kenya."	Barack Obama said [that] his father's family **comes** from Kenya.
The archaeologist said, "Mount Everest **is called** Chomolungma by the Tibetans."	The archaeologist said [that] Mount Everest **is called** Chomolungma by the Tibetans.
The student said, "Helena **is** happy with her grade."	The student just said [that] Helena **is** happy with her grade.

6. Reporting verbs are generally in the past; however, when the reporting verb is in the present, the verb in the noun clause remains in the present.

DIRECT SPEECH	INDIRECT SPEECH
In every speech, the president of the International Cycling Union **says**, "Cheating is harming the sport of professional cycling."	In every speech, the president of the International Cycling Union **says** [that] cheating **is** harming the sport of professional cycling.

7. Some pronouns and possessive adjectives change when direct speech changes to indirect speech. Notice how the pronouns and the possessive adjective change in the following examples.

DIRECT SPEECH	INDIRECT SPEECH
Hillary Rodham Clinton said, "**I** have worked persistently on issues relating to women, children, and families."	Hillary Rodham Clinton said [that] **she** had worked persistently on issues relating to women, children, and families.
Barack Obama said, "**My** father's family comes from Kenya."	Barack Obama said [that] **his** father's family comes from Kenya.
The CEO announced, "**We** can reduce the company's debt."	The CEO announced [that] **they** could reduce the company's debt.

8. Time and place words change when direct speech changes to indirect speech.

DIRECT SPEECH	INDIRECT SPEECH
now	then, at that time
today	that day
tomorrow	the next day, the following day, a day later
tonight	that night
yesterday	the day before, the previous day
yet	by that time
last week/month/year	the week/month/year before, the previous week/month/year
this week/month/year	that week/month/year
next week/month/year	the next/following week/month/year
this	that
these	those
here	there

Direct: *The children asked, "Why is the moon so bright* **tonight***?"*

Indirect: *The children asked why the moon was so bright* **that night***.*

Direct: *The student said, "I cannot study* **here today** *because there is too much noise."*

Indirect: *The student said [that] he couldn't study* **there that day** *because there was too much noise.*

9. Indirect speech can also be used to report questions and imperatives.

	DIRECT SPEECH	INDIRECT SPEECH
Yes/no questions: In indirect speech, yes/no questions use *if* or *whether or not.*	The patient asked, "**Do I need** to take these pills every day?"	The patient asked **if he needed** to take those pills every day. The patient asked **whether or not he needed** to take those pills every day.
***Wh-* questions:** In indirect speech, *wh-* questions use statement word order.	"**Where is your identification**?" an airport security officer questioned.	An airport security officer questioned **where her identification was**.
Imperatives: In indirect speech, imperatives change to infinitives or noun clauses.	"**Read** the article on page 27, but **do not answer** the questions at the end," the teacher remarked.	The teacher told the students **to read** the article on page 27 but **not to answer** the questions at the end. OR The teacher told the students that they **had to read** the article on page 27, but they **didn't have to** answer the questions at the end. (*Should, ought to, had better,* and *have to* are possible in this form.)

10. *Say* and *tell* are the most common reporting verbs that are used to introduce other people's thoughts, ideas, or words. The listener (a noun or pronoun) must follow the verb *tell*, while mentioning the listener is not necessary with the verb *say*. Do not use *to* after *tell*; however, if you mention the listener with *say*, you must use *say to*.

Every day our English teacher says **[to the class]** *how important good grammar is.*

My boss told **me** *that I could expect a promotion within the next year.*

not

My boss told to me that I could expect a promotion within the next year.

See pages 118–119 for a longer list of verbs that can be used to introduce other people's thoughts, ideas, and words.

Circle the sentence that forms and uses indirect speech correctly.

1. **(a)** The student assistant told to me that Dr. Romy was not holding office hours today.

   (b) The student assistant told me that Dr. Romy was not holding office hours today.

2. **(a)** My boss asked me what I had learned at the conference.

   (b) My boss asked me what had I learned at the conference?

3. **(a)** My roommate's father inquired why I wasn't in class.

   (b) My roommate's father inquired why aren't you in class?

4. **(a)** The professor told the class they will be having a test tomorrow.

   (b) The professor told the class they would be having a test the next day.

5. **(a)** The last census stated that the U.S. population had grown by 500 million.

   (b) The last census stated that the U.S. population has grown by 500 million.

FORMING SENTENCES WITH QUOTATIONS

Quotations are the exact words of a speaker or writer and must have quotation marks (" ") around the sentence or partial sentence that is quoted. The quotation must have the exact spelling and punctuation of the original. The speaker or writer of the quoted material is called an outside source; a source is used in academic writing to support and strengthen the ideas or argument in a piece of writing.

1. Introduce a quotation with the full name of the source (the writer or speaker of the quoted material) and other related information such as the title of the article or book and a reporting verb such as *say* or *write*. The next time the same source is mentioned, use only his or her last name. Use a pronoun if the same source is used again close by.

   "The Kansas City School District is a very upsetting situation," **said Larry Orbach**, *a Washington University sociologist who has studied the district for years.*

   To **Orbach**, *the lesson from Kansas City is clear: Money can't buy good schools.*

   He *says this is especially obvious in "urban districts where poverty leaves many children ill-prepared to learn."*

2. The source's name may appear at the beginning, middle, or end of a quotation with the correct punctuation; notice where commas, periods, and quotation marks are placed in the following examples.

   Franklin Delano Roosevelt said, "We *have nothing to fear but fear itself."*

   (Use a comma after the reporting verb and begin the quotation with a capital letter if it is a complete sentence. The period at the end of the sentence goes inside the quotation marks.)

"We have nothing to fear but fear itself," **said Franklin Delano Roosevelt**.

(Use a comma at the end of the quotation even if the quotation is a complete sentence. Place the comma inside the quotation marks.)

"We have nothing to fear," *said* **Franklin Delano Roosevelt,** *"but fear itself."*

(If you place the source's name in the middle of the quotation, use a comma to separate the quotation at a place where there is a natural pause. Follow the source's name with another comma and continue the quotation with quotation marks. Do not begin the second half of the quotation with a capital letter because it is not the beginning of a new sentence. End the quotation with a period inside the quotation marks.)

3. The reporting verbs that introduce quotations can be in the simple present or the simple past. The general guideline is if the quoted material refers to the past, the reporting verb is usually in the past. If the quoted material refers to the present, the reporting verb is usually in the present.

In Writing from A to Z *the authors* **contend**, *"Editing and revising* **should be done** *in separate readings of the manuscript, because revising* **focuses** *on the larger elements of content and organization and editing* **focuses** *on sentences and words."*

(The quotation states a widely held belief and is in the present, so the reporting verb *contend* is in the simple present.)

Studies on smoking **found**, *"when heavy smokers* **decreased** *their smoking by half for two or three months, levels of certain tobacco-related toxins in their bodies* **did not go down**.*"*

(The results discussed in the quotation were found in the past and the quotation is in the past, so the reporting verb *found* is in the simple past.)

In 1965 Martin Luther King, Jr. **said**, *"I* **have** *a dream that one day this nation* **will rise up** *and* **live out** *the true meaning of its creed."*

(The reporting verb *said* is in the past because the quotation is from the past even though the quoted material is in the present and future.)

4. Quotations may also be introduced with a signal phrase, such as *according to,* or an introductory clause. Notice where commas, periods, and quotation marks occur.

According to Dr. Beth Besch, *"Children don't understand that their words can harm others, so they must be taught that words can hurt just like hitting or pushing."*

(Use a comma after the signal phrase and begin the quotation with a capital letter if it is a complete sentence. The period at the end of the sentence goes inside the quotation marks.)

Dr. Beth Besch discusses teaching children the significance their words have: *"Children don't understand that their words can harm others, so they must be taught that words can hurt just like hitting or pushing."*

(Use a colon after the introductory clause if it is a complete sentence and begin the quotation with a capital letter if it is also a complete sentence. Place the period at the end of the sentence inside the quotation marks.)

WRITING TIP

Stating the source of a quotation is not only necessary but also strengthens the writer's ideas in the readers' eyes and gives the reader the opportunity to refer to the writer's original sources.

5. A quotation does not always have to include the full sentence taken from the original source. Many times it is preferable to use only a portion of the source's original words and to blend them into your own sentence. However, the source's original meaning must not be changed in any way when only part of the quoted material is used.

In The Resourceful Writer, *William Barnwell and Robert Dees suggest using "quotations to support or further explain your points, but do not depend on them too heavily."*

Writing is used to express your point of view on a particular topic; however, academic writing relies on "balancing your voice with the ideas, research, and theories of other people," according to Holten and Marasco in Mastering Academic Writing.

6. A quotation of more than forty words begins on a new line and does not have quotation marks. The entire quotation should be indented one-half inch.

According to Mary Fitzpatrick in Engaging Writing,

> *in academic writing you are required to identify the source of your information. Whenever you use outside sources—whether you are quoting or paraphrasing a single sentence or summarizing an entire book—you need to identify the source of your information and give credit to the author.*

7. Use square brackets ([ ]) around words that you add to the quotation for grammatical accuracy or clarification.

In the textbook Great Essays, *the authors explain that essays are "a short collection of paragraphs that present facts, opinions, and ideas on topics* **[that]** *can range from a description of a visit to Disney World to an argument about capital punishment."*

As a piece of writing develops, "the method that a writer chooses **[to write the essay]** *is based on the topic."*

8. Use ellipsis (. . .) if you must remove words from the quotation.

Although the rules for punctuation "have changed throughout the centuries . . . by the eighteenth and nineteenth centuries, the system we know was generally in place," writes Martha Kolln in Rhetorical Grammar.

USING SENTENCES WITH QUOTATIONS

1. Always explain the background or significance of quoted material. Do not simply place a quotation in your paper and expect the reader to understand it.

The Juvenile Justice System was not developed simply to imprison children who had committed crimes. It was established to reform juvenile criminals because society believes that these children can still "be developed into productive citizens instead of adult criminals." Therefore, American society provides the necessary help to these at-risk children.

not

The Juvenile Justice System was established for criminals under eighteen years of age. "At-risk children must be developed into productive citizens instead of adult criminals." It is the responsibility of American society to provide the necessary help to these at-risk children.

WRITING TIP

Plagiarism occurs when a writer takes personal credit for another person's words or ideas by not referring to that person and not using quotation marks. The rules for plagiarism are different in each country. Consult your instructor or a book on the research process to make sure that you are following the guidelines for avoiding plagiarism.

2. Reporting verbs that introduce quotations and indirect speech have specific meanings. Be sure to use the correct verb for the meaning you want to convey.

- To introduce most quotations use: *analyze, announce, consider, describe, discuss, explain, express, illustrate, inform, mention, note, notify, observe, point to, present, recognize, remark, report, say, state, suggest, tell,* or *write.*

  The paper **reported** *that the FBI is analyzing "evidence that was obtained at the crime scene."*

- To introduce quotations that provide additional information use: *add, continue, further discuss, further explain, further illustrate, further state, later express, later mention,* or *later observe.*

  The president **further illustrated** *his belief in the need for government to help support childcare by "increasing funding by 15 percent in the coming year."*

- To introduce quotations that present opinions use: *acknowledge, advise, agree, argue, assert, believe, caution, charge, claim, contend, criticize, declare, demand, deny, disagree, emphasize, hold, indicate, imply, maintain, object, oppose, propose, support, think, urge,* or *warn.*

  In Dean Schulberg's editorial, he **contends** *that "grade inflation must come to an end if a university degree is to mean anything."*

- To introduce quotations that are questions or to question an established belief use: *ask, inquire, question,* or *wonder.*

  At the end of his presentation, Professor Jeffries **wondered** *whether or not parents today have "the knowledge of how to discipline their children" when they received little discipline themselves as youngsters.*

- To introduce quotations that respond use: *agree, answer, concur, disagree, dispute, reply,* or *respond.*

  The committee **agrees** *with earlier findings that "welfare programs only work in a limited number of cases."*

- To introduce quotations that conclude use: *conclude.*

  The paper **concludes** *with a plea for "further research to fully answer the questions we still have regarding the need for a space program."*

The reporting verbs *say*, *state*, *tell*, and *write* are neutral verbs. They do not express your opinion or an evaluation of the speaker's words. However, other verbs and adjectives do show your opinion about what the speaker says. Choose reporting verbs and adjectives carefully to express the meaning that you intend.

	VERBS	ADJECTIVES
Strong ↓ Weak	command, demand, order, require insist, urge ask, request advise, prefer, recommend propose, suggest	critical, crucial, essential, urgent, vital best, imperative, necessary important, recommended desirable, preferable advisable

3. The title of the publication where the quotation comes from must be included. <u>Underline</u> or *italicize* the titles of books, magazines, and newspapers and put quotation marks around the titles of articles and short stories.

> *If people want to lose weight, doctors have regularly recommended exercise, but new research shows exercise "can stimulate hunger [which] causes us to eat more," according to "Why Exercise Won't Make You Thin" in* Time.

4. Include the credentials of the source. This strengthens the quotation. A source's credentials include present or past job titles, university degrees, or published works.

> *Young people in Sweden are picking new names for their married life that come from older family names or that they may even make up themselves. Eva Brylla,* **the director of research at the Institute of Language and Folklore in Uppsala**, *reported "the practice of changing names had been around for more than a century in Sweden . . . but in recent years, the trickle of name changing has become a flood."*

5. Always include information about where you found a quotation or idea that you expressed in direct or indirect speech. This is called citing your sources. Complete source information is usually listed on a separate page of sources at the end of the paper. Details about the source such as year of publication or page number are given in abbreviated form in parentheses near the quotation or indirect speech. The Modern Language Association (MLA) and American Psychological Association (APA) provide the most commonly used rules on how to cite sources. Ask your teacher which method he or she requires and refer to an MLA or APA style guide for the specific rules. MLA and APA guidelines are also posted on the Internet. The following example sentences illustrate just a few of the differences between MLA and APA.

> MLA: *Ann Raimes wrote that when you use other people's ideas, "you can quote exact words, you can report in indirect speech, or you can use your own words entirely in a paraphrase or summary" (156).*

> APA: *According to Ann Raimes (2004), "When you record what people say or write, you can quote exact words, you can report in indirect speech, or you can use your own words entirely in a paraphrase or summary" (p. 156).*

WRITING TIP

Although quotations strengthen the ideas or argument in your writing, do not overuse them. Readers want to read what you have to say. Quotations are most effective when they are used sparingly.

Self Check 3

Circle the sentence that forms and uses quotations correctly.

1. **(a)** In his book *Timeless Healing*, Dr. Herbert Benson states that in future generations changing our "genetic predispositions and instinct" may be possible, but ". . . the implications and ethics of this is another matter altogether."

   (b) In his book *Timeless Healing*, Dr. Herbert Benson talks about changing our behavior by changing our genes. "We cannot yet change our genetic predispositions and instincts by behavioral decisions alone."

2. **(a)** According to Dr. Kerry Ressler of Emory University, "In a lot of very impoverished, high-violence neighborhoods, we see high rates of trauma, much like we see in veterans."

   (b) According to Dr. Kerry Ressler of Emory University, "in a lot of very impoverished, high-violence neighborhoods, we see high rates of trauma, much like we see in veterans".

3. **(a)** "Because housing is the single largest expenditure for most households, housing affordability has the potential to affect all domains of life that are subject to cost constraints, including health."

   (b) Lance Freeman, author of *America's Housing Crisis: A Contract Unfulfilled*, states that "housing affordability has the potential to affect all domains of life . . . including health."

4. **(a)** The valedictorian announced we are the next generation, and our fathers' world is about to become ours during the graduation ceremony.

   (b) "We are the next generation," the valedictorian announced during the graduation ceremony, "and our fathers' world is about to become ours."

5. **(a)** During the accident investigation, the driver claimed she "was tired and didn't realize that I had driven out of my lane and into oncoming traffic."

   (b) During the accident investigation, the driver claimed she "was tired and didn't realize that [she] had driven out of [her] lane and into oncoming traffic."

WRITING TIP

Three Quick Steps to Using Quoted Material:

1. Introduce the quotation with the source's name and give the quotation. Do not simply place the quotation into your paper without giving credit to the original source.

2. Blend the quoted material into your own sentence whenever possible.

3. Add an additional sentence that explains or clarifies the quotation. It is your responsibility to help your readers understand the importance of the quotation.

EDITING PRACTICE

1. *Put a check (✓) next to the sentences that use noun clauses and indirect and direct speech correctly. Correct the sentences that have errors. There may be more than one way to correct some errors.*

_____ **1.** Education prepares students for what will they face in the real world.

_____ **2.** How society creates new slang terms are an area of study at the university.

_____ **3.** After several burglaries at the same address, the police advised that the resident lock his front door at all times.

_____ **4.** The public transportation system assured passengers that it would be prepared for possible terrorist attacks in the future.

_____ **5.** La Leche League tells to new mothers that breastfeeding is the best choice for both mothers and babies.

_____ **6.** The growing world population is harming the environment is troubling.

_____ **7.** Where we all came from is the main focus for many anthropologists.

_____ **8.** In the mid-twentieth century, behaviorist B.F. Skinner stated that positive and negative reinforcement had shaped the behavior of his research subjects.

_____ **9.** It was decided that the best action for the defendant would be a plea bargain.

_____ **10.** In 47 BCE, Julius Caesar comments on one of his victories, "I came, I saw, I conquered."

_____ **11.** In her opening argument, the attorney reminded the jury "divorces were illegal in many states only sixty years ago."

_____ **12.** According to the U.S. Welfare System, most states offer "basic aid such as health care, food stamps, child care assistance, unemployment, cash aid, and housing assistance."

2. *Read the following paragraph. Complete the paragraph with the correct structure.*

Maturity is a term used in psychology to indicate

_____ to the environment. An
    1. how does a person respond / how a person responds

appropriate response is a sign of maturity. Maturity is usually learned and

not determined by one's age. In many cases, however, society uses age, not

maturity, to decide _____ to perform
       2. when people are able / when are people able

certain tasks such as driving, drinking, and joining the military. In fact, the

U.S. Juvenile Justice System was established in 1904 based on the belief that maturity develops with age. According to Julian Mack, founder of Chicago's first juvenile court, young people _____

3. did / do

not always make good decisions because they are immature, but they

_____ more easily reformed than adults.

4. were / are

Yet, much debate still remains _____ a

5. whether / Ø

relationship between maturity and age exists. This becomes a dilemma for parents who wonder when a child is responsible enough to be allowed some freedom. When boys' voices begin to change or when they start to grow a beard _____ a sign of physical

6. is / are

maturity. However, _____ parents

7. what do psychologists tell / what psychologists tell

is to look for signs of social development before they allow their children more freedom. This advice is supported by new imaging techniques that reveal the teenage brain continues to develop well beyond puberty and

_____

8. "is a very complicated and dynamic arena, one that is not easily understood." / "the

_____

teenage brain is a very complicated and dynamic arena, one that is not easily understood."

Therefore, when parents finally decide _____

9. that their child / why their child

deserves some of the freedom that comes with age, there is no guarantee that the child will act with appropriate maturity. _____

10. John MacNaughton believes,

_____

"Maturity begins to grow when you can sense your concern for others outweighing your

_____

concern for yourself." / Ultimately, the true sign of maturity is "when you can sense your

_____

concern for others outweighing your concern for yourself," according to author and poet

_____

John MacNaughton.

3. *In the following paragraph, six of the underlined noun clauses are not correct. Correct the errors.*

In the 2004 State of the Union address, George W. Bush stated, "America is the land of the second chance, and when the gates of the prison open, the path ahead should lead to a better life." **(1)** <u>That the United States is the land of second chances</u> is a sentiment held by many Americans who feel their country is eager to help those who have made mistakes or are seeking new opportunities. The juvenile justice system is one example of **(2)** <u>how society insists youth be given additional chances.</u> Frequently, the second chance for juveniles is education, which a prominent U.S. senator calls **(3)** <u>"I believe education is a capital investment in our future."</u> The juvenile justice system is also based on the belief **(4)** <u>that the state has the responsibility to take care of all children in need of protection.</u> Another example of a second chance that American society offers is the community college system. In community colleges across the country, adults are encouraged to return to school to learn new skills and teenagers are able to strengthen their academics before

transferring to universities. Community college mission statements often declare that increasing educational opportunities (5) <u>are</u> a primary goal.

(6) <u>The community college system admits anyone over 18 years of age</u> shows its willingness to provide a second chance to all. In addition, many immigrants look at a new life in the United States as a second chance for themselves as well as their children. Many past immigrants frequently said (7) <u>that they will not have had the same opportunities in their home countries.</u> (8) <u>How do people choose to use their second chances</u> is never certain. (9) <u>The truth is when some take advantage of a second chance,</u> while others ignore these opportunities. Although this idea is not tolerated in many countries of the world, one of the strongest beliefs in the United States is (10) <u>that people deserve the chance to succeed even if they initially fail.</u>

4. *The following paragraphs have ten errors in the use of noun clauses and direct and indirect speech. Find and correct the errors. There may be more than one way to correct some errors.*

While the term "generation gap" became popular in the 1960s, the division between children and their parents existed long before that time and still continues today. Young people maintain that their parents do not understand them, and parents believe that their children show them little respect. In other words, what children and parents value are very different. Why does the generation gap exist is not easily explained.

In previous decades, parents said that the generation gap develops from young people challenging their parents' old-fashioned beliefs; in the twenty-first century, both older and younger generations say that they are separated by skills and abilities. In addition to this, some members of the older generation tell to their children and grandchildren that they have lost an appreciation of tradition and culture. What the children value in modern culture is not the same as what do their traditional parents value.

Children in earlier generations promised themselves that they will not allow the generation gap to develop in their own families, yet the gap has continued to exist. That the generation gap is pushing away their own children are shocking to this generation of parents. Many parents feel like writer J.B. Priestly, who said, "there was no respect for youth when I was young, and now that I'm old, there is no respect for age." Although the formation of the generation gap may be inevitable, to slow its growth it is essential that a child listens to his or her parents. Counselors additionally recommend that parents are available to listen to their children at all times.

WRITING TOPICS

Most academic essays and research papers require an introduction with a strong thesis statement. The body paragraphs that follow the introduction support the thesis with references to outside sources. These outside sources might be summarized, quoted, or paraphrased. Notice how the following body paragraph, which was taken from a longer piece of writing, includes a topic sentence, a body with support from outside sources, and a concluding sentence. Use this paragraph as a model when you write about one of the following topics.

Study the use of noun clauses and direct and indirect speech in the following student paragraph. Underline each of the noun clauses in this paragraph.

Like other traditional cultures, the Poles have many superstitious traditions that are unique to them and perhaps a few of the countries surrounding Poland. One of the most interesting traditions involves a *kominiarz*, or chimney sweeper. In Poland, chimney sweepers dress in all black uniforms accompanied by a black cap similar to a small top hat. Although they are much rarer than they used to be, chimney sweepers can still be easily spotted on the street in their unique attire. When a chimney sweeper is sighted, it is customary to "hold a button and make a wish," according to Polimex, an international Polish travel agency.[1] The Poles hope that this will bring them good luck. Stella Kmiecik, an American woman raised by her immigrant Polish parents, recalls how her father believed that he had been blessed with good fortune because he had seen a *kominiarz* on the street the day that he had boarded the boat to his new country.[2] How the tradition of button holding began has been forgotten, but the *kominiarz* has been a longtime symbol of good fortune and health in the home.

Choose one topic below and write at least one paragraph. Find an outside source to support the ideas that you present in your writing. Use several quotations, noun clauses, and indirect speech. After you complete your first draft, concentrate on editing your work. Keep in mind the editing practice from this chapter.

1. Some superstitions you may be familiar with are "Don't let a black cat cross your path" and "If you break a mirror, you will have seven years of bad luck." What other superstitions do you know? What culture or country are they from? How did these superstitions develop? Do you or does anyone you know believe in them?

2. Describe the person whom you admire most in the world. This can be a world figure or someone closer to home, such as a parent or neighbor. Explain what this person has done and said to deserve your admiration.

Go to page 183 for more practice with noun clauses and direct and indirect speech.

[1] "Polish Superstition," Polimex Travel, accessed July 14, 2011, http://travel.polimex.com/en/content/polish-superstition.

[2] Stella Kmiecik as reported to Allison L. Morgan.

Writing Concisely

GRAMMAR FOCUS

Academic writing is generally very concise. This means that it contains only the necessary words to express an idea clearly. If it is possible to say something in three words, then the writer uses three words, not five or ten words. One way to write concisely is to reduce adjective and adverb clauses, and another way is to avoid wordy language. For example, *today* or *now* is just as effective as *at the present time*. Notice how the sentence below can be written concisely by omitting unnecessary words.

WORDY LANGUAGE	First of all, it is interesting that people who are poor or middle class donate more money to charities or nonprofit organizations than people who are wealthy donate to charities or nonprofit organizations.
CONCISE LANGUAGE	Interestingly, poor and middle-class people donate more to charities than wealthy people do.

Pretest

Check your understanding of concise writing. Put a check (✓) next to the sentences that are written correctly with concise language.

_____ 1. Children need to be taught to apologize and to say that they are sorry for their actions when they do something wrong.

_____ 2. Running for Congress, his objectives were very clear.

_____ 3. The Emperor Penguin, the largest species of penguin, is found in Antarctica.

_____ 4. The newspaper editorial strongly rejected with firm opposition the decision to reduce the police force.

_____ 5. Sentences containing errors in structure and function are unacceptable.

_____ 6. The lighting designer uses the color amber to create highlights, and she uses the color blue to create shadows.

_____ 7. Cosmetic companies use celebrity endorsements more often than clothing companies use celebrity endorsements.

_____ 8. The cardiologist prescribed a new drug for her patient. The new drug will help control high blood pressure.

_____ 9. The Puritans modeled their lives on religion and hard work.

_____ 10. Ignoring the coming hail storm, the teenager left his car on the driveway.

Notice how two sentences in the following paragraph have been rewritten concisely. Study the two underlined sentence parts. Concisely rewrite this wordy language.

Lately ~~in the last few years,~~ green exercise has become a topic of interest as well as research. Green exercise refers to physical activity that people do in a natural environment. For example, hiking in the mountains, running along the seashore, and walking in a forest are all forms of green exercise. People say that they have greater mental clarity and energy **after hiking through the woods than** ~~after they hike through the woods than when they~~ **walking in the city** ~~walk in the city~~. Studies also found that <u>patients that are in the hospital</u> recover more quickly if they can see nature from their hospital windows. Some researchers believe that plants release chemicals into the air that produce some of <u>the good benefits</u> that people report after green exercise. In addition, some of these advantages may take only fifteen to twenty minutes to experience.

REDUCING CLAUSES

One way to write concisely is to reduce some of the clauses in your writing. Both adjective clauses and adverb clauses can be reduced to phrases. A clause is a group of words with both a subject and a verb; a phrase is a group of words that does not have both a subject and a verb.

Reducing Adjective Clauses

Remember that adjective clauses describe or identify a noun and can be restrictive or nonrestrictive. A restrictive adjective clause supplies necessary information to identify the noun it modifies. A nonrestrictive clause supplies additional information not necessary to identify the noun.

> Restrictive adjective clause: *Stories* **that describe futuristic scientific and technological changes** *are called science fiction.*
>
> Nonrestrictive adjective clause: Gulliver's Travels**, which Jonathan Swift wrote,** *is considered one of the first pieces of science fiction.*

1. To reduce an adjective clause that contains a *be* verb, omit *that, who(m)*, or *which* and the *be* verb.

   Adjective clause: *The professor **who is lecturing** teaches political science.*

   Reduced to adjective phrase: *The professor **lecturing** teaches political science.*

   Adjective clause: *Theories **that are proven with evidence** become facts.*

   Adjective phrase: *Theories **proven with evidence** become facts.*

   Adjective clause: *The Rock and Roll Hall of Fame, **which is on the waterfront in Cleveland**, Ohio, displays rock-and-roll memorabilia.*

   Adjective phrase: *The Rock and Roll Hall of Fame, **on the waterfront in Cleveland, Ohio,** displays rock-and-roll memorabilia.*

2. Some adjective clauses can be reduced to appositives. An appositive is an adjective phrase that follows a noun and renames the noun. To reduce an adjective clause to an appositive, omit *that, who(m)*, or *which* and the *be* verb.

   Adjective clause: *Hawaii, **which is the fiftieth state**, has over 400,000 indigenous people.*

   Appositive: *Hawaii, **the fiftieth state**, has over 400,000 indigenous people.*

   Adjective clause: *Ronald Reagan, **who was the fortieth president of the United States**, was also a movie actor.*

   Appositive: *Ronald Reagan, **the fortieth president of the United States**, was also a movie actor.*

3. To reduce an adjective clause that contains *be* + adjective, omit *that, who(m)*, or *which,* then move the adjective before the noun that it modifies.

   Adjective clause: *An essay **that is well written** takes hours to compose.*

   Adjective: *A **well-written** essay takes hours to compose.*

4. If the adjective clause does not contain a *be* verb, omit *that, who(m)*, or *which* and change the verb to the *–ing* form. This reduction is only possible when *that, who,* or *which* is the subject of the adjective clause.

   Adjective clause: *An essay **that supports its thesis** is well written.*

   Adjective phrase: *An essay **supporting its thesis** is well written.*

   Adjective clause: *The essay **that the students wrote on homelessness** was due last week.*

   not *The essay writing on homelessness was due last week.* (In this sentence, the word *students* is the subject of the clause; therefore, this clause cannot be reduced.)

5. *Who(m), that,* or *which* can be deleted from an adjective clause only if it is not the subject of the clause.

   *The article **that The New York Times published yesterday** identified CIA spies.* (*That* is the object of the clause. *The New York Times* is the subject of the clause.) →

   *The article **The New York Times published yesterday** identified CIA spies.*

   *Professional and college athletes **who(m) children idolize** can often be bad role models.* (*Who[m]* is the object of the clause. *Children* is the subject of the clause.) →

   *Professional and college athletes **children idolize** can often be bad role models.*

WRITING TIP

One of the main characteristics of academic writing is conciseness, but many native speakers of English feel adjective clauses that are not reduced are the most formal.

Formal: *The scientists whom the Nobel committee recognizes receive over a million dollars.*

Less formal: *The scientists who the Nobel committee recognizes receive over a million dollars.*

Less formal: *The scientists that the Nobel committee recognizes receive over a million dollars.*

Least formal: *The scientists the Nobel committee recognizes receive over a million dollars.*

Self Check 1

Circle the sentence that reduces adjective clauses correctly.

1. **(a)** *Kira-Kira*, was written by Cynthia Kadohata, won the Newbery Medal in 2005.

   (b) *Kira-Kira*, written by Cynthia Kadohata, won the Newbery Medal in 2005.

2. **(a)** The award honoring film excellence in Australia is called the Australian Film Institute Award.

   (b) The award honors film excellence in Australia is called the Australian Film Institute Award.

3. **(a)** The athlete well prepared won the competition.

   (b) The well-prepared athlete won the competition.

4. **(a)** People who love words are good at games like Scrabble, Boggle, and Scattergories.

   (b) People love words are good at games like Scrabble, Boggle, and Scattergories.

5. **(a)** Bisquick is a quick mix for biscuits was introduced in 1931 by General Mills.

   (b) Bisquick, a quick mix for biscuits, was introduced in 1931 by General Mills.

Reducing Adverb Clauses

Remember that adverb clauses describe relationships between events such as time, location, reason, and contrast. Adverb clauses are dependent clauses introduced by subordinating conjunctions.

> **After Candi Lightner's daughter was killed by a drunk driver,** *she founded MADD (Mothers Against Drunk Drivers).*

> *MADD is one of the most highly supported nonprofit organizations* **because** *it* **has substantially reduced the number of drunk drivers.**

1. The subject of an adverb clause and an independent clause must be the same to reduce the adverb clause.

   Adverb clause and independent clause with the same subject: *After the researcher collected bacteria specimens, he had to cancel the research project.*

   Adverb clause reduced to adverbial phrase: **After collecting bacteria specimens,** *the researcher had to cancel the research project.*

Adverb clause and independent clause with different subjects: *After the researcher collected bacteria specimens, the research project was cancelled.*

not

After collecting bacteria specimens, the research project was cancelled.

(The two clauses in this sentence have different subjects, so the adverb clause cannot be reduced.)

2. Adverb clauses of time (introduced with *after, before, since, until, when, whenever,* or *while*) can be reduced to adverbial phrases by omitting the subject and changing the verb in the adverb clause to the *–ing* form. When the verb in an adverb clause is in the past, it may change to the *–ing* form or to *having +* past participle.

   Adverb clause: **While researchers monitor bacterial levels**, *they can become very sick.*

   Adverbial phrase: **While monitoring bacteria levels**, *researchers can become very sick.*

or

   Monitoring bacteria levels, *researchers can become very sick.*

   Adverb clause: **After he had compiled the results**, *the sociologist presented his findings.*

   Adverbial phrase: **After having compiled the results**, *the sociologist presented his findings.*

or

   After compiling the results, *the sociologist presented his findings.*

or

   Having compiled the results, *the sociologist presented his findings.*

NOTE: The sentence "Compiling the results, the sociologist presented his findings" expresses the idea that both of these actions took place at the same time, while the other three sentences express the idea that the researcher compiled the results and later presented his findings.

3. Adverb clauses of cause (introduced with *as, because, since,* or *due to the fact that*) can be reduced to adverbial phrases by omitting the subordinating conjunction and the subject and changing the verb to the *–ing* form. When the verb in an adverb clause is in the past, it may change to the *–ing* form or to *having +* past participle.

   Adverb clause: **Because Turkey maintains a strong economy**, *it remains politically stable today.*

   Adverbial phrase: **Maintaining a strong economy**, *Turkey remains politically stable today.*

   Adverb clause: **As Turkey experienced an unstable government for many years**, *it was not a popular tourist destination in the past.*

   Adverbial phrase: **Having experienced an unstable government for many years**, *Turkey was not a popular tourist destination in the past.*

or

   Experiencing an unstable government for many years, *Turkey was not a popular tourist destination in the past.*

4. Adverb clauses of concession (introduced with *although, despite, though, in spite of,* or *while*) can be reduced to adverbial phrases in one of several ways.

(a) Omit the subject of the adverb clause and change the verb to the *–ing* form. When the verb in the adverb clause is in the past, it may change to the *–ing* form or to *having* + past participle.

Adverb clause: **Although health care expenses cost little prior to the 1970s,** *they were paid for by employer-provided health insurance.*

Adverbial phrase: **Although costing little prior to the 1970s,** *health care expenses were paid for by employer-provided health insurance.*

or

Although having cost little prior to the 1970s, *health care expenses were paid for by employer-provided health insurance.*

(b) Omit the subject and the *be* verb of the dependent clause.

Adverb clause: **Though health insurance is expensive for employers,** *it is a necessary expense.*

Adverbial phrase: **Though expensive for employers,** *health insurance is a necessary expense.*

(c) Omit the subject and the stative verb of the dependent clause.

Adverb clause: **While employees feel lucky to have health insurance,** *they also feel trapped by this benefit.*

Adverbial phrase: **While lucky to have health insurance,** *employees also feel trapped by this benefit.*

5. In the passive voice, adverb clauses of time, cause, and concession can be reduced.

(a) In adverb clauses of time, omit the subject and change the *be* verb in the adverb clause to the *–ing* form. When the verb in the adverb clause is in the past, it may change to the *–ing* form or to *having* + past participle.

Adverb clause of time: **After Haiti was severely damaged in the 2010 earthquake,** *it needed millions of dollars in aid.*

Adverbial phrase: **After being severely damaged in the 2010 earthquake,** *Haiti needed millions of dollars in aid.*

or

After having been severely damaged in the 2010 earthquake, *Haiti needed millions of dollars in aid.*

(b) In adverb clauses of cause, omit the subordinating conjunction, the subject, and the *be* verb in the adverb clause.

Adverb clause of cause: **Since much of the aid was misused by government officials,** *it did not help the ordinary citizens.*

Adverbial phrase: **Misused by government officials,** *much of the aid did not help the ordinary citizens.*

(c) In adverb clauses of concession, omit the subject and the *be* verb in the adverb clause.

Adverb clause of concession: **Even though many Haitians were injured in the earthquake,** *they feel hopeful for their future.*

Adverbial phrase: **Even though injured in the earthquake,** *many Haitians feel hopeful for their future.*

6. Some subordinating conjunctions that introduce clauses of concession or cause can be reduced to prepositional phrases.

Adverb clause of concession: **Despite the fact that Kodak was dominant in the photography business,** *it has faced financial trouble recently.*

Prepositional phrase: **Despite Kodak's dominance in the photography business,** *it has faced financial trouble recently.*

Adverb clause of concession: **In spite of the fact that photography has quickly evolved from film to digital,** *it has remained a popular hobby for amateur photographers.*

Prepositional phrase: **In spite of the quick evolution from film to digital photography,** *photography has remained a popular hobby for amateur photographers.*

Adverb clause of concession: **Although Kodak is not the company's official name,** *it is more frequently used than Eastman Kodak Company.*

Prepositional phrase: **Although not the company's official name,** *Kodak is more frequently used than Eastman Kodak Company.*

Adverb clause of cause: **Because Kodak was able to change from film to digital technology,** *it has remained competitive in the photography business.*

Prepositional phrase: **Because of its ability to change from film to digital technology,** *Kodak has remained competitive in the photography business.*

7. Avoid dangling participles in reduced adverb clauses. A dangling participle occurs when the subject of the dependent clause is not the same as the subject of the independent clause. To reduce an adverb clause, the subject of both clauses must be the same.

(a) not *Flying into a storm, turbulence rocked the plane back and forth.*

(b) reworded *Flying into a storm, the plane was rocked back and forth by turbulence.*

Sentence (a) says that the turbulence was flying into the storm.

(a) not *While driving down the street, a dog ran in front of my car.*

(b) reworded *While driving down the street, I saw a dog run in front of my car.*

Sentence (a) says the dog was driving down the street.

(a) not *Drawn with charcoal and oil, the artist displayed his newest painting.*

(b) reworded *Drawn with charcoal and oil, the newest painting was displayed by the artist.*

Sentence (a) says the artist was drawn with charcoal and oil.

Self Check 2

Circle the sentence that reduces adverb clauses correctly. Remember that not all sentences with adverb clauses can be reduced.

1. **(a)** Because of high property taxes, the schools in this district are good.

   (b) Because of the property taxes are high, the schools in this district are good.

2. **(a)** Since credit card companies experience so much fraud, interest rates are high on credit cards.

   (b) Experiencing so much fraud, interest rates are high on credit cards.

3. (a) Before was elected, the senator was a schoolteacher.

(b) Before being elected, the senator was a schoolteacher.

4. (a) Although three feet of snow, the storm was not the biggest of the season.

(b) Although dropping three feet of snow, the storm was not the biggest of the season.

5. (a) Surgeons perform surgery, they must wash their hands for a minimum of five minutes.

(b) Whenever performing surgery, surgeons must wash their hands for a minimum of five minutes.

WRITING TIP

Although contractions such as *don't, it's,* and *there's* make writing more concise by combining words, they are considered informal and are not always appropriate in academic writing. In spoken English, nouns and verbs are often contracted, as in the sentences, "The essay'll be finished soon" and "The teacher'd had enough of the students' complaints." These types of contractions are not appropriate in formal written English.

OTHER TECHNIQUES FOR WRITING CONCISELY

1. Use pronouns to write concisely and to link ideas between sentences.

> *A group of transfer students asked a counselor to help them with their college applications.* **This** *resulted in much stronger responses to all the questions on the applications.*

not *A group of transfer students asked a counselor to help them with their college applications. Asking a counselor to help them with their college applications resulted in much stronger responses to all the questions on the applications.*

> *University admissions officers recommend writing a personal statement that tells a story.* **They** *want to see an applicant's experiences through vivid examples.*

not *University admissions officers recommend writing a personal statement that tells a story. Admissions officers want to see an applicant's experiences through vivid examples.*

WRITING TIP

Do not use a pronoun if it results in ambiguity—that is, if it is not clear who or what the pronoun refers to.

If my parents discuss household chores with my brothers, **my brothers** *usually get mad.*

not *If my parents discuss household chores with my brothers, they usually get mad.*

They is ambiguous. It is unclear whether it refers to *parents* or *brothers.*

---

2. Avoid repetition that occurs when a sentence repeats the same information using different words.

Wordy: *Because it is so expensive in price to house prisoners, the state prison system is going broke.*

Concise: *Because it is so expensive to house prisoners, the state prison system is going broke.*

Wordy: *Musicians need to practice often at least once every day.*

Concise: *Musicians need to practice often.*

3. Choose one or two words to make a point rather than a longer string of words. For example, *because of the fact that* can be reduced to *because*, and *true facts* can be replaced with *facts*. Use this list of common phrases to make your writing more concise. A more complete list appears in Appendix 6.

WORDY	CONCISE
all of a sudden	suddenly
as a matter of fact	in fact
at the present time	now
at the same time	simultaneously
but nevertheless	but *or* nevertheless
each and every	each *or* every
good benefit	benefit
in my opinion I think	in my opinion *or* I think
in order to	to
on the other hand	conversely
past history	history
square in shape	square
write down	write

4. Reduce comparative sentences when possible.

- Omit the verbs or nouns that are repetitive in the second half of the comparison.

    Private universities are usually smaller than public universities ~~are~~.

    The public university's budget was cut more than the private university's ~~budget~~.

not *The public university's budget was cut more than the private university.*

The correct statement compares the public university's budget to the private university's budget. The incorrect statement compares the budget to the university. Make sure that the same item is being compared in both parts of the statement.

- Replace possessive adjectives and their nouns with possessive pronouns.

    The tuition at our college increased more than the tuition at ~~their college~~ theirs.

    Your university has fewer students than ~~my college~~ mine.

- Do not state information in the second half of the comparison that is understood.

    Colleges are currently dealing with higher expenses and smaller budgets ~~than in the past~~.

It is clear that this is a comparison between the past and present; therefore, it is not necessary to include this information in the second part of the comparison.

5. Use ellipsis to avoid unnecessary repetition. Ellipsis occurs when part of a sentence is left out. In the following examples only the auxiliary verb is repeated.

    The army will leave the occupied country, and the marines will ~~leave the occupied country~~ too.

    The soldiers are looking forward to returning home, just as the sailors are ~~looking forward to returning home~~.

6. Combine sentences with different kinds of conjunctions, clauses, and punctuation to make writing more concise.

> Wordy: *One of the characteristics of academic writing is strong vocabulary.* **The reason why is because** *specific and vivid language expresses a writer's ideas very clearly.*
>
> Concise (with subordinating conjunction): *One of the characteristics of academic writing is strong vocabulary* **because** *specific and vivid language expresses a writer's ideas very clearly.*
>
> Wordy: *To support all of a writer's claims, strong academic writing must use evidence.* **The evidence can include quotations, statistics, or anecdotes.**
>
> Concise (with adjective clause): *To support all of a writer's claims, strong academic writing must use evidence* **that can include quotations, statistics, or anecdotes***.*
>
> Wordy: *Good writers are able to* **write strong thesis statements. They can also develop topic sentences that support the thesis. Finally, they think critically** *to provide support that is logical and convincing.*
>
> Concise (with coordinating conjunction and parallel structure): *Good writers are able to* **write strong thesis statements, develop topic sentences that support the thesis, and think critically** *to provide support that is logical and convincing.*
>
> Wordy: *In the final stage of the writing process, writers proofread their essay.* **Proofreading means that the writers** *look at grammar, mechanics, punctuation, and usage.*
>
> Concise (with punctuation): *In the final stage of the writing process, writers proofread their essay*; **they** *look at grammar, mechanics, punctuation, and usage.*
>
> Wordy: *The first stage in the writing process is prewriting.* **Prewriting includes** *brainstorming, free writing, diagramming, making lists, and outlining.*
>
> Concise (with punctuation): *The first stage in the writing process is prewriting*: *brainstorming, free writing, diagramming, making lists, and outlining.*
>
> Wordy: *Good writing involves several stages.* **An effective paper goes through a multistage process that begins with prewriting and ends with editing.**
>
> Concise (with punctuation): *Good writing involves several stages*—**from prewriting to editing**—**if the paper is going to be effective.**

NOTE: See Appendix 4 in *Grammar for Writing 2* for more information on punctuation.

WRITING TIP

Use parentheses sparingly. Parentheses are used only to clarify information or provide missing information in a sentence. If you are using parentheses for other reasons, the information inside the parentheses should be included in the sentence outside of the parentheses or omitted.

Circle the sentence that uses the concise form.

1. **(a)** ESL students should always edit for grammar daily before they submit their work

   (b) ESL students should always edit for grammar before they submit their work.

2. **(a)** The students at private universities pay higher student fees than the students at public universities pay.

   (b) The students at private universities pay higher student fees than the students at public universities.

3. **(a)** The architect's new designs were often triangular in shape.

   (b) The architect's new designs were often triangular.

4. **(a)** People should check their account balances and credit card statements regularly. This is important so that identity theft can be caught early.

   (b) People should check their account balances and credit card statements regularly. Checking account balances and credit card statements is important so that identity theft can be caught early.

5. **(a)** Medical information is strictly confidential between doctors and patients, as legal information is strictly confidential between lawyers and clients.

   (b) Medical information is strictly confidential between doctors and patients, as legal information is between lawyers and clients.

EDITING PRACTICE

1. *Put a check (✓) next to the sentences that use concise language correctly. Correct the sentences that have errors or do not use the concise form. There may be more than one concise form.*

____ **1.** The student talking during class disrupted the lecture.

____ **2.** Working to meet an important deadline, the students stayed up all night.

____ **3.** Finishing the revision of his essay, the paper looked well written.

____ **4.** In conclusion, the author concludes by summarizing her main arguments.

____ **5.** Many companies try to attract customers by using endorsements as a marketing technique.

____ **6.** Congress plans to deliberate the matter at a later date in the future.

____ **7.** Children that are different from their peers can experience bullying.

____ **8.** While preparing to defend her dissertation, the graduate student received a job offer at a prestigious university.

_____ **9.** At the present time, researchers are now on the brink of finding a cure for baldness.

_____ **10.** The winning chef cooked more creatively than the second-place chef.

_____ **11.** Quite suddenly, the general launched an unexpected surprise attack on the enemy.

_____ **12.** It is important for children to have lots of exercise, and children also need at least eight to ten hours of sleep each night.

_____ **13.** Sociology is the study of all aspects of society: social class, social mobility, religion, law, and deviance.

2. *Read the following paragraph. Complete the paragraph with the concise forms.*

From 1770 through 1810, the world

was experiencing "revolutionary fever."

_____

    1. This / This "revolutionary fever"
hit several parts of the world,

_____ France,

    2. among those being / including
Haiti, Latin America, and the British colonies of

North America. Suffering oppression and tyranny

from _____,

    3. their governments / the governments who held supreme power over them
revolutionaries rose up _____ for

              4. in rebellion to fight / to fight
essential social, economic, and political changes. These revolutionaries

made it clear that the revolutions they led were for the good of the

_____ and not for personal gain.

    5. people as a whole / people

_____, the revolutionaries chose one

    6. In order to do this / To do this
person as the "liberator-hero," who was given much of the credit for

the successes of the revolution. Some examples of liberator-heroes are

Paul Revere in the United States, Simón Bolivar in Latin America, and

François Dominique Toussaint-Louverture in Haiti. This liberator-hero

became a _____; through this

    7. necessity that was centralized / centralized necessity

person, the revolutionaries gained the support of the people. Though not

_____ revolutions achieved victory, the
8. all of the / all the

liberator-heroes remained, and the ideals and reasons for the revolutions

lived on through _____. For generations, the
9. the liberator-heroes / them

stories of these _____ were told.
10. glorified heroes / heroes that were glorified

3. *In the following paragraph, the ten underlined words, phrases, and clauses can be written more concisely. Rewrite these in fewer words. There may be more than one concise form.*

There are <u>thousands of different languages</u> <u>that are recognized</u> in the
                                1   2

world today, from English, to Chinese, to Swahili, to Sioux. <u>As a matter of fact</u>,
                                                                      3

within English, there are several different varieties. <u>Americans speak a</u>
                                                                  4

<u>different form of English than the British speak</u>, and <u>the British certainly speak</u>

<u>English differently than Jamaicans and Australians speak English</u>. Additional
                                                        5

differences exist between written and spoken language, gestures and body

language, as well as international sign language and its regional variations. It

is hard to label language by <u>any one, single definition</u>. Even animals have
                                               6

their <u>own individual</u> version of language. Meercats, <u>which are small rodent-</u>
      7   8

<u>like mammals</u>, are able to warn their family of danger. <u>When bumblebees</u>
                                                            9

<u>dance a specific foot pattern</u>, bumblebees tell other bees where food is located.

While some people may consider this type of communication to be an

instinct rather than a language, simply because humans cannot understand

<u>a language</u> does not mean the language does not exist.
 10

4. *In the following paragraph, there are ten places where concise language has not been used. Find the wordy sentences or sentence parts and replace them with more concise language. There may be more than one way to correct some of the wordy language.*

World War II was unlike any other wars that were fought in the past; it was an all-encompassing, total war. Not only was each and every country involved in the struggle, but all aspects of life—economic, political, and social—were affected.

The war took front and center economically, politically, and socially. All citizens became nationalistic patriots to the country and its allies. But nevertheless, all parties that were involved paid a high price. Civilians made as many sacrifices to help the war effort as the soldiers made to help the war effort; this is what an all-encompassing war means. Civilians who remained on the homefront lived with the rationing of cars, gasoline, bicycles, footwear, food, nylon, and firewood. When young men enlisted in the military, young men knew that they might be killed, but it was worth the sacrifice for their country. Finally, at the end of World War II, soldiers returned home, but the country and world were changed forever.

WRITING TOPICS

Most academic essays and research papers require an introduction with a strong thesis statement. The body paragraphs that follow the introduction support the thesis with references to outside sources. These outside sources might be summarized, quoted, or paraphrased. Notice how the following body paragraph, which was taken from a longer piece of writing, includes a topic sentence, a body with support from outside sources, and a concluding sentence. Use this paragraph as a model when you write about one of the following topics.

Notice how the student of the following paragraph writes concisely. Study how the underlined sentences express the writer's ideas using only the necessary words.

When facing budget cuts, school administrators often first eliminate high school theater classes. However, they are some of the most beneficial courses a student can take. Theater classes encompass several areas that build a foundation for future careers: lighting design, management, acting, construction, architecture, cosmetology, and psychology. Furthermore, theater allows students to face and overcome one of the most common fears: stage fright. Whether acting on a stage, presenting in a classroom, interviewing for a job, or making a speech at a friend's wedding, we are all going to be the center of attention someday. Having the ability to feel at ease during these situations is vital to our success. Also, participating in fine arts classes allows students to excel in other areas. Robert DeBruyn of the Saddleback Valley Unified School District states that "participation in the arts enhances learning in other areas, including the development of higher-order thinking skills and awareness of the world we live in."[1] The arts give students a new perspective on life and even on people. Theater can definitely make a difference in a high school student's life.

Choose one topic below and write at least one paragraph. Find an outside source to support the ideas in your writing. Practice reducing clauses and using other techniques from the chapter to write concisely. After you complete your first draft, concentrate on editing your work. Keep in mind the editing practice from this chapter.

1. Recently, companies that sell health insurance have considered increasing the cost of insurance for people who lead unhealthy lives and decreasing the cost for people who make healthy choices. Do you think it is fair to penalize some people for unhealthy lifestyle choices and to reward others for healthy choices? Why or why not?

2. All high school students study subjects such as math, English, and history but are allowed to choose other classes like foreign languages, physical education, and photography as electives. What high school classes are the most important for students to take to be prepared for the future? Why do you believe these are the most important?

Go to page 186 for more practice with writing concisely.

....

[1] Robert DeBruyn, "The Importance of Visual and Performing Arts," Saddleback Valley Unified School District, accessed July 14, 2011, http://www.svusd.org/p_subject.asp?sid=14100.

GRAMMAR FOCUS

Good writers choose their words with care. They know that the vocabulary in a piece of writing is just as important as the grammar and that academic writing requires formal, specific, and vivid language. This chapter will help you develop appropriate vocabulary and avoid inappropriate vocabulary for academic writing. Notice how the information in the following sentences is the same, yet one sentence is more academic because of the vocabulary choices.

INFORMAL WRITING	The cop put up with the rude kids because the bottom line is he wanted to develop trust between the police and the community.
ACADEMIC WRITING	The police officer tolerated the rude children because he ultimately wanted to develop trust between the police and the community.

Pretest

Check your understanding of academic vocabulary. Put a check (✓) next to the sentences that use academic vocabulary.

_____ **1.** The guy was acting totally bizarre when the cop stopped him.

_____ **2.** The jury wanted to look over the evidence before deciding on the defendant's guilt or innocence.

_____ **3.** Many large corporations have struggled to remain in business during the economic downturn.

_____ **4.** An army officer must maintain good standing within his unit to increase his rank.

_____ **5.** Especially, Mother's Day is the busiest day of the year for restaurants.

_____ **6.** Businesses must provide special entrances and facilities for the disabled.

_____ **7.** The judge put off the court date to a later time.

_____ **8.** Following long droughts, farmers find their land is as hard as a rock and difficult to cultivate.

_____ **9.** There remain many faraway galaxies for astronomers to study.

_____ **10.** The archaeologists provided irrefutable proof of an early civilization.

Notice how the writer has revised the vocabulary in the following paragraph.
Replace the underlined words or phrases with academic vocabulary.

        exists
There is a debate over how best to handle the growing epidemic of childhood and teenage obesity. Traditional solutions include reducing calories, especially those from fat and sugar, increasing physical activity, and participating in behavioral therapy. Health care providers, dieticians, and government officials <u>make up</u> the group of people who support these traditional solutions. This group <u>says</u> that the established methods are the only way for weight loss to be long term and safe for children and
                                          emerged
teenagers. Another side to this debate has recently ~~come on the scene~~. This group
               perform
supports a procedure in which doctors ~~do~~ surgery that limits the amount of food obese children and teenagers can eat. They <u>say</u> that surgery is the most effective solution to help these children and teenagers lose weight and decrease or eliminate problems with heart disease, high blood pressure, sleep disorders, and diabetes. However, some people are opposed to this approach. Although obesity carries many health risks, these people believe that the risks involved with surgery are too high. They argue that even a <u>one in a million</u> chance of an unsuccessful outcome of surgery is too high for a child or teenager to face.

USING ACADEMIC VOCABULARY

1. Idioms and clichés are expressions that have been overused in spoken and written English. Because these expressions are so commonplace, they have become ineffective; they should be used sparingly in formal writing.

Clichés to avoid	
as a matter of fact	green with envy
better late than never	hard as a rock
bored to death	in this day and age
the bottom line	last but not least
cold as ice	a matter of life and death
to cost an arm and a leg	one in a million
the early bird catches the worm	out of this world
easier said than done	put all your eggs in one basket
every cloud has a silver lining	the whole nine yards

2. *There is, there were,* and *there will be* are used by writers to show that something exists. *There* is most commonly followed by the verb *be*. Because *there* is an empty word, it is generally considered better to place the real subject first in academic writing.

    Good: **There is** *a Latin dance exercise called Zumba.*

    Better: **A Latin dance exercise is** *called Zumba.*

    Better: **Zumba is** *a Latin dance exercise.*

    Good: **There were** *Zumba dance programs in Colombia before they spread worldwide.*

    Better: **Zumba dance programs were** *in Colombia before they spread worldwide.*

    While placing the real subject first is often preferred, in formal writing *there* can be followed by verbs other than *be* that make writing sound academic. These verbs fall into two categories:

    • verbs that show existence: *exist, live, remain*

      There exist *few exercise programs that are as fun as Zumba.*

    • verbs that show direction: *come, go, approach*

      At the same time that Zumba was becoming popular, **there came** *into the United States many other dance exercises from overseas.*

3. Slang is considered very informal and inappropriate for academic writing. Some commonly used slang in spoken English to avoid in academic writing includes *awesome, buck, cool, cop, dude, guy, hang out, kid, OK, ripped off, stuff, thing,* and *totally.* Because slang changes rapidly, the list of unacceptable slang terms must be continually updated.

4. Two-word verbs or phrasal verbs are generally more informal than one-word verbs. Choose one-word verbs whenever possible in academic writing. The following list provides one-word synonyms for some informal two-word verbs.

TWO-WORD VERBS	ONE-WORD SYNONYMS
bring about	produce
bring up	raise
come back	return
cut down	reduce
do away with	eliminate
drop by	visit
drop out	quit
figure out	determine
get together	meet
go away	leave *or* depart
leave out	omit
let down	disappoint
let out	release
look over	examine
make up*	compose
point out	indicate
put in	insert
put off	postpone
put up with	tolerate
sign up for	register
stir up	evoke
take back	return
think over	consider
turn down	decline
turn in	submit

Make up and *compose* are frequently used in their passive forms (*be made up of / be composed of*). Although *be composed of* is not a one-word verb, it is generally considered more formal than *be made up of*.

5. Choose specific verbs to express your opinion or someone else's opinion. The neutral verb *say* or *said* is appropriate in some situations, but other verbs such as *inquire, demand, claim, maintain, emphasize,* and *illustrate* can express your meaning more precisely. See page 118 for a list of other verbs that express opinion.

6. Academic writing is unbiased. This means that it is fair; it does not show support for one group, person, or belief more than another. Academic writing should avoid language that may offend anyone who reads it.

- Do not mention race, ethnicity, disability, or age in a piece of writing when it is not relevant to the topic. However, when this information is necessary for the content of an essay, use vocabulary that does not offend a specific group. For example, referring to someone as *disabled* is appropriate, but referring to him or her as *crippled* is offensive; *elderly* is an appropriate adjective, while *old* may be inappropriate; and calling someone a *Native American* is appropriate, but *Indian* is not often used. When referring to different races or ethnicities in the United States, it is common today to attach the term *American* to the name: for example, *African-Americans, Korean-Americans, Chinese-Americans.*

NOTE: A good dictionary will label some words "offensive." These words should not be used in academic writing.

- Do not use sexist language. Rather than using the masculine pronouns *he, him,* and *his,* it is common to use *he/she, him or her,* or *his or her;* however, this can become awkward if overused. Use plural pronouns to avoid this problem.

Sexist language: *An accountant must pass a state exam before he receives his license.*

Acceptable language: *An accountant must pass a state exam before he or she receives his or her license.*

Most appropriate language: *Accountants must pass a state exam before they receive their license.*

Use gender-neutral language whenever possible.

SEXIST LANGUAGE	GENDER-NEUTRAL LANGUAGE
businessman	businessperson, manager, executive
chairman	chairperson, chair
cleaning woman	cleaner, cleaning staff
fireman	firefighter
freshman	first-year student
mailman	mail carrier, letter carrier, or postal worker
maintenance man	maintenance worker, maintenance staff
mankind	humans, human beings, people
manpower	personnel
policeman	police officer
salesman or saleswoman	salesperson, sales associate, sales clerk
seamstress	tailor
stewardess	flight attendant
waiter or waitress	waitperson or server
watchman	guard
workman	worker

7. Quantifiers occur frequently in academic writing and can be classified as formal or informal. By choosing quantifiers carefully, your writing will sound more academic.

Formal: *much, many, numerous, few, a few, little, a little, a number of, the number of, a great deal of, a small amount of*

Informal: *lots of, a lot of, tons and tons of, a bunch of, a tiny bit of, hardly any, plenty of, buckets of, pretty much, a really lot of*

WRITING TIP

Use a dictionary that labels words as formal, informal, slang, scientific, and so on. This will help you to choose vocabulary that is appropriate for the type of writing that you are doing.

Self Check 1

Circle the sentence that uses academic vocabulary.

1. (a) Mailmen are required to deliver the mail regardless of weather conditions.

   (b) Postal workers are required to deliver the mail regardless of weather conditions.

2. (a) Substantial increases in fuel prices are costing consumers hundreds of dollars monthly.

   (b) Big rises in gas prices are costing consumers an arm and a leg.

3. (a) Old people catch colds and the flu more easily than young people.

   (b) The elderly are more susceptible to colds and the flu than the young.

4. (a) Many immigrants from underdeveloped countries claim to be economic refugees.

   (b) Many immigrants from poor countries say they are economic refugees.

5. (a) Many kids throughout the world make less than a buck a day by picking through garbage.

   (b) Many children throughout the world earn less than a dollar a day by combing through garbage.

COLLOCATIONS

Collocations or word partners are composed of two or more words that usually appear together. When words are appropriately paired, they sound correct. For example, the most common verb that pairs with *crime* is *commit*: *A teenager **committed a crime** last night*. It is not natural to say, *A teenager did a crime last night* because *do* and *crime* do not collocate. By using collocations correctly, writing sounds academic, natural, and precise. Some common collocations used in academic writing follow.

1. To write about your research or to discuss another person's research:

Verb Phrases	
research suggests	to play a central role
to challenge a theory/evidence	to propose a theory
to establish a connection	to provide evidence
to go into great detail	to set out arguments
to make a decision	to strongly defend
to offer supporting evidence	to support the claim

Noun Phrases	
a concise summary	a powerful/weak argument
a key factor	irrefutable proof

2. To write about causes and effects:

Noun Phrases	
a cause for concern	a(n) likely/unlikely cause
a harmful effect	an adverse effect
a major cause of	an immediate cause
a negative effect	an underlying cause

Verb Phrases	
to be caused by something	to have a major impact on something
to be responsible for something	to lead to something
to feel the effects of something	to result in something

3. To express comparisons and contrasts:

Comparison Verb Phrases
to be the same as
to have something in common with

Comparison Noun Phrases
a further similarity

Comparison Transitions	
as well as	in the same way
just as	on a similar note

Contrast Verb Phrases
to be different from
to be earlier/later than
to be/have more/less than

Contrast Noun Phrases
another difference

Contrast Transitions
in contrast
on the other hand

WRITING TIP

To use language effectively in your writing, it is important not only to learn the meaning of new words but to practice using them in context. Do more than memorize the definition of a single word; notice the words that occur around the new word or its collocations. It's also helpful to practice the word's pronunciation and begin using the word in spoken and written sentences.

Self Check 2

Circle the sentence that uses collocations correctly.

1. **(a)** Many people believe that Pablo Picasso is responsible for the popularity of the Cubist art movement in the early twentieth century.

   (b) Many people believe that Pablo Picasso is responsible to the popularity of the Cubist art movement of the early twentieth century.

2. **(a)** University engineering programs will soon feel the adverse effects of poor elementary and high school science curriculum.

   (b) University engineering programs will soon feel the bad effects of poor elementary and high school science curriculum.

3. (a) Investigators quickly made a connection between talking on the phone while driving and an increased number of car accidents.

(b) Investigators quickly established a connection between talking on the phone while driving and an increased number of car accidents.

4. (a) Research suggests that good therapists must have sympathy for their patients but remain detached from them.

(b) Research says that good therapists must have sympathy for their patients but remain detached from them.

5. (a) Teenagers generally have more in common with their parents than they would like to believe.

(b) Teenagers generally are more in common with their parents than they would like to believe.

COMMONLY CONFUSED WORDS AND PHRASES

Some common words and phrases are frequently used incorrectly. Study the following list of the definitions and forms of these commonly confused words and phrases.

Nouns, Verbs, and Adjectives

accept (verb) to receive

> *The student* **accepted** *the $5,000 scholarship.*

except (preposition) exclude or omit something

> *The scholarship pays for everything* **except** *books.*

cloth (uncountable noun) fabric such as cotton, wool, and silk

> *The kimono is made of very expensive* **cloth**.

clothes (plural noun) things that people wear such as shirts, pants, and dresses

> *The child's* **clothes** *are hand-me-downs from her older sister.*

concern (verb) to feel worried or upset

> *Environmental problems* **concern** *young people today.*

to be concerned about (verb + past participle + preposition) to feel worried or upset

> *Young people* **are concerned about** *environmental problems.*

emphasize (verb) to present an idea or opinion in a strong way

> *The instructor* **emphasized** *the importance of grammar.*

to put emphasis on (verb + noun + preposition) to present an idea or opinion in a strong way

> *The instructor* **put** *a lot of* **emphasis on** *verb forms.*

face (verb) to deal with or be affected by a difficult situation

> *The public* **faces** *new crime issues every day.*

to be faced with (verb + past participle + preposition) to deal with or be affected by a difficult situation

> *The public* **is faced with** *new crime issues every day.*

passed (verb, simple past) to go by a person, place, or thing

> *The students* **passed** *the library on the way to the coffee shop.*

past (adjective) before now

> *During the* **past** *year, she graduated and found a good job.*

past (noun) the time that existed before the present

> *The* **past** *is what historians study.*

past (preposition) up to and beyond

> *The students walked* **past** *the library on the way to the coffee shop.*

Conjunctions and Transitions

beside (preposition) next to

> *He sat* **beside** *the groom's family at the ceremony.*

besides (transition) in addition to

> **Besides** *working together, they also take a class in the evening.*

especially (adverb) to emphasize something

to introduce an example

> *Billions of greeting cards are sold annually on special occasions,* **especially** *Christmas, Valentine's Day, and Mother's Day.*

to modify an adjective; used like *very*

> *Handmade greeting cards are* **especially** *popular now.*

not   *Especially, handmade greeting cards are popular now.*

for example used before examples to support a previous statement

as a transition

> *Many autocratic governments have been overthrown.* **For example**, *East Germany, the Soviet Union, Tunisia, and Egypt used to be governed by a single ruler with unlimited power.*

as a prepositional phrase

> *Many countries have overthrown autocratic governments,* **for example**, *East Germany, the Soviet Union, Tunisia, and Egypt.*

not   *Many countries have overthrown autocratic governments. For example, East Germany, the Soviet Union, Tunisia, and Egypt.*

WRITING TIP

Do not use abbreviations in academic writing. Use full words such as *until* and *through*, not the abbreviations *till* and *thru*.

Self Check 3

Circle the sentence that uses commonly confused words or phrases correctly.

1. (a) The country's rising debt concerns all citizens, especially the younger generations.

   (b) The country's rising debt is concerned about all citizens, especially the younger generations.

2. (a) Children and teenagers may be the victims of bullying because of their clothes.

(b) Children and teenagers may be the victims of bullying because of their cloth.

3. (a) Several U.S. presidents did not come from wealthy families, for example, Lincoln, Truman, Grant, and Clinton.

(b) Several U.S. presidents did not come from wealthy families. For example, Lincoln, Truman, Grant, and Clinton.

4. (a) Madame Curie excepted the Nobel Prize for chemistry in 1911.

(b) Madame Curie accepted the Nobel Prize for chemistry in 1911.

5. (a) The Oscar nominee has won her place besides some of the greatest names in Hollywood.

(b) The Oscar nominee has won her place beside some of the greatest names in Hollywood.

WRITING TIP

Do not settle for the first word that you put down on paper. Use the revision process to select words that express your meaning as precisely as possible.

EDITING PRACTICE

1. *Put a check (✓) next to the sentences that use academic vocabulary. Correct the sentences that have errors or do not use academic vocabulary. There may be more than one academic form.*

_____ **1.** The defendant stated that the bottom line was his innocence.

_____ **2.** To relieve stress, people must eliminate all the things in their mind and relax.

_____ **3.** Because they are trained as paramedics, firefighters respond to all emergency calls even if they are not fire related.

_____ **4.** The salesperson past the sales quota earlier than expected.

_____ **5.** Many fashion designers demand their apprentices work first as tailors.

_____ **6.** Paleontologists believe that before "Lucy" there existed no human-like life forms.

_____ **7.** New companies won't generally go public till their stock is highly valued.

_____ **8.** Civil rights laws outlaw discrimination against women and minority groups such as African-Americans.

_____ **9.** Labor union representatives brought up the topic of workplace safety.

_____ **10.** The meteorologist went into great detail about how wind affects atmospheric temperatures.

_____ **11.** In this day and age, employers expect employees to understand how to navigate social networking sites.

_____ **12.** Airport security emphasizes on arriving two hours before the flight departure time.

2. *Read the following paragraph. Complete the paragraph with the correct vocabulary choice for formal academic writing.*

While most people don't often

_____ the
    1. think over / consider

important role that lighting plays in the arts, it

is a complex field that is worthy of attention.

One area where lighting plays an especially large

role is in theater. If special lighting techniques

_____ ,
    2. were done away with / were eliminated

at the end of a performance most audiences would

_____ feeling as if something were missing.
    3. go away / leave

Therefore, the stage lighting designer _____
                                     4. makes / has

many important decisions regarding the look and feel of a

theater production. To do this, lighting designers rely on three

_____ : PAR (parabolic aluminized
    5. things / lighting instruments

reflector), ERS (ellipsoidal reflector spotlight), and Fresnel. All three

_____ , but each has unique qualities.
    6. are used a lot / are commonly used

Of the three lighting instruments, the ERS is the most frequently used

_____ . The ERS has
    7. because it can do many different things / because of its versatility

the ability to shift from hard to soft focus; this means that it ranges from a

spotlight beam to a gentle wash of light. The PAR and Fresnel have focusing

capability, but neither can _____ a drastic
                           8. produce / bring about

lighting shift like the ERS. The ERS also produces light that has shape and

texture. By _____ a special filter, the lighting
9. putting in / inserting

designer can use ERS to create a shape such as a heart or star or a texture

such as water or leaves. These are some of the key lighting methods lighting

designers use to _____ a particular mood in a
10. stir up / evoke

stage production and help the audience feel the production as well as see and

hear it.

3. *In the following paragraph, replace the underlined words and phrases with more academic vocabulary. There may be more than one academic word or phrase that is appropriate in each sentence.*

Many people <u>say</u> that birds are the most interesting and diverse of all
¹

animals because of their many shapes, sizes, colors, and forms. If we <u>look at</u>
²

their prevalence in modern culture, penguins may be considered the most

interesting of all birds. Penguins have been the subject of <u>lots of</u> books,
³

movies, cartoons, and songs. <u>A big cause of</u> this is their very formal look with
⁴

the black "tuxedo jacket" and "white shirt." Another intriguing <u>thing about</u>
⁵

penguins is their habitat. While most birds make their home in warm <u>spots</u>,
⁶

the penguin is one of the few birds that lives in the cold regions of the world.

<u>Getting together</u> in large groups, many types of penguins can be found in
₇
sub-Antarctic regions of the world, <u>like</u> the islands south of Australia,
₈
Tasmania, New Zealand, and South Africa. Although most penguins are

incapable of flight, they migrate just as other bird species do, but they do this

on foot for as many as 60 miles. This is an arduous trek for them, but it is

<u>a matter of life and death</u> that they reach their breeding grounds every spring.
₉
Although penguins do not fly, they have wings that are an <u>awesome</u> tool for
₁₀
swimming, for they function much like flippers. Even for people who don't

like birds, penguins are a popular animal. Several <u>big factors</u> in their
₁₁
popularity may be the penguins' human-like appearance, monogamous

relationships, and the tremendous struggles that they go <u>thru</u> each year to
₁₂
bring their babies into the world.

4. *In the following paragraph, there are ten places where academic vocabulary
has not been used. Find the informal or incorrect language and replace it with
academic vocabulary. There may be more than one way to correct some of the
informal language.*

The nuclear reactor explosion in Chernobyl, Ukraine, may be the worst

nuclear accident in history. In 1989, the Chernobyl facility experienced a

bunch of steam explosions that let out radioactive material into the air. As

a matter of fact, the radiation caused by the explosions spread thru several

countries and affected tons and tons of people. This accident made a really big

impact on the nuclear industry, leaving it nearly stagnant for twenty years.

Only recently has public approval for nuclear energy begun to come back

as a result of dependence on expensive fossil fuels from unstable regions of

the world. In addition, nuclear energy is being promoted as the eco-friendly

energy source. Today, nuclear power makes up nearly twenty percent of the world's energy, and energy consumption is pretty much expected to double over the next few decades. However, since the nuclear disaster that Japan experienced after the earthquake on March 11, 2011, most experts advise against putting all of our eggs into one basket and recommend developing a variety of energy sources instead.

WRITING TOPICS

Most academic essays and research papers require an introduction with a strong thesis statement. The body paragraphs following the introduction support the thesis with references to outside sources. These outside sources might be summarized, quoted, or paraphrased. Notice how the following body paragraph, which was taken from a longer piece of writing, includes a topic sentence, a body with support from outside sources, and a concluding sentence. Use this paragraph as a model when you write about one of the topics on page 156.

Study the academic vocabulary in the following student paragraph. Underline the vocabulary that you consider academic.

It is commonly known that people do not always tell the truth for a variety of different reasons, but research tells us that the truth is withheld from health care providers more often than from any other group. This can be extremely dangerous, as doctors cannot accurately diagnose a patient's illness unless they understand all the habits and symptoms of the patient. According to Barbara Morgan, a registered nurse on the cardiac floor of St. Luke's Hospital in St. Louis, Missouri, patients often lie about their diet and exercise habits because they are embarrassed and often "feel as though doctors and nurses are judging them."[1] Because of this, patients often state that they engage in unhealthy activities much less often than they actually do. "When we ask a patient how often he or she engages in an unhealthy activity, we usually multiply that number by three," Morgan reports.[2] Covering up the truth occurs even more frequently with adolescent and teenage patients because they fear the reactions of their parents as well as of health care providers. What patients forget, however, is that all medical information is strictly confidential and cannot be released to anyone unless the patient signs a waiver that grants the health care provider permission to do so. Although most forms of lying carry risks, lying to health care providers can have especially dangerous consequences.

[1] Barbara Morgan, discussion with Allison L. Morgan, March 1, 2011.

[2] Morgan, discussion.

Choose one of the topics below and write at least one paragraph. Find an outside source to support the ideas that you present in your writing. Use vocabulary appropriate for academic writing. After you complete your first draft, concentrate on editing your work. Keep in mind the editing practice from this chapter.

1. Write about the reasons that people lie. Discuss whether or not it is important to be honest all of the time.

2. Online classes are becoming more common. What are some of the differences between online classes and classroom-based learning? Is one type of instruction better than the other? Why or why not?

Go to page 188 for more practice with academic vocabulary.

Extra Editing Practice

EDITING FOCUS

Use the following pieces of writing to practice editing for grammar points that you have focused on in the previous chapters. When you edit your own writing, it is important to look for a variety of grammatical errors; therefore, each exercise in this chapter requires that you edit for more than one type of grammatical structure.

WRITING TIP

It is important to always get feedback on the writing that you do. Work with your teacher or a tutor to help you locate and correct errors in your writing. This will help to reinforce correct grammar and good writing techniques. If you don't get instruction from your teacher or a tutor, you may reinforce bad grammar and writing habits.

NOUNS, DETERMINERS, AND SENTENCE STRUCTURE

Edit carefully for errors in the use of nouns, determiners, and sentence structure. There are ten errors in the following paragraph.

Many cultures around the world they have days that are set aside to honor deceased family members. In Mexico and a small amount of other Central and South American countries, this day is called *Dia de los Muertos* or the Day of the Dead. It is time when people remember their ancestors by

building private altars that honor them and gathering at their gravesites. In addition, picnics with the ancestor's favorite foods and beverages. This celebration was originally held in mid-summer during the Aztec month of *Miccailhuitontli* (pronounced mick-hail-wheat-tont-lee). After the Spanish conquest of Mexico, Spanish priests moved a holiday to coincide with Christian holiday, All Hallows Eve, the Day of the Dead is now observed on the first two days of November. Celebrations similar to the Day of the Dead are observed in European countries with catholic traditions and in the Philippines. The Bon Festival in Japan, Chuseok in Korea, the Ching Ming Festival in China, and Gai Jatra in Nepal are also celebrations that honor deceased ancestors. The traditions vary by region and by degree of urbanization; however all cultures see these holidays as the time of celebration rather than as a time of sadness.

USING NOUN CLAUSES AND WRITING CONCISELY

Edit carefully for five errors in the use of noun clauses. Continue to edit for conciseness by reducing two clauses and rephrasing three instances of overly wordy language.

Language helps define who are we and provides the first impression people have of us. What a total stranger says establish the gender, age, and culture of that person. For example, language such as "chick" for girl, "dude" for boy, "cool" for good, and "fine" for attractive clearly distinguishes one generation from the next. In addition to identifying speakers as members of different age groups, language can also reveal a speaker's gender. Frequently, males use different words and expressions than the words and expressions that females use. Culture also plays a role in the language we choose. When people meet in Chinese society, they ask each other if they have eaten yet. This is a traditional greeting that came from a past historical time of poverty and starvation. In many Western countries, this greeting would seem strange for the reason that the most common greeting in the West is to ask how is a person. With the rapid spread of English worldwide, people might wonder is all language going to become the same. Linguists know that no language can completely fight outside influence, but it is essential that language continues to define the unique characteristics of gender, age, and culture.

VERB TENSE, SENTENCE STRUCTURE, AND AGREEMENT

Edit carefully for errors in the use of verb tense, sentence structure, and agreement. There are ten errors in the following paragraph.

The Slow Movement had begun at the end of the twentieth century as a general protest against the fast pace of life. The Slow Food Movement was the first group to gain notoriety in the late 1990s. It was originally a movement against fast food, but has developed to promote traditional and regional foods that are grown organically and enjoyed in the company of other people. The Slow Food Movement has given birth to Slow Gardening, Slow Travel, and Slow Parenting to name a few. The most recent addition to this list is the Slow Computer Movement. A group that advocates for slower computer connections. As crazy as this may sound in a world that wants Internet connections to take seconds or even nanoseconds, this group yearned for the bygone era of dial-up connections. Because so much of people's time is spent on computers nowadays, the Slow Computer Movement believes that by slowing their computers, people will improve our lives. Slow Computer advocates are believing that slow computer connections increase productivity by eliminating useless Internet surfing, develop better relationships by forcing face-to-face communication, and improve mental outlook by allowing people time to think and plan while waiting for computer searches. The Slow Computer movement as well as all the other Slow Movements are evidence that society experiences a reduced quality of life because too much desire for speed, one solution is to gain an appreciation for life by slowing it down according to the supporters of the Slow Movement.

VERB TENSE, PASSIVE VOICE, AND ACADEMIC AND CONCISE VOCABULARY

Edit carefully for errors in the use of verb tense and the passive voice. Also, academic and concise vocabulary have not been used. There are ten errors in the following paragraph.

Approximately five pounds of trash per day is generate by every American. This trash eventually ends up at a landfill. It is shocking to see the amount of trash that is dumped into landfills in a whole entire year. To deal with all the trash in the United States, they're over 3,000 landfills. Over time, this trash problem gets worse and has the potential to be crazy harmful to our environment and our planet. While numerous methods are used to prevent leakage from landfills, toxic chemicals are eventually absorbing into the soil and water around them. To combat this, other forms of waste management have been becoming increasingly widespread. Of these, incineration and recycling are the most effective. Modern incinerators use pollution-controlling devices to capture the toxic emissions and are regulated by strict federal and state laws. While incinerators are helpful because they destroy waste rather than store it, recycling is beneficial for it reuses waste again. As a matter of fact, if everyone recycled, incinerators and landfills would cease to exist.

MODALS, DETERMINERS, AND AGREEMENT

Edit carefully for errors in the use of modals, determiners, and agreement. There are ten errors in the following paragraph.

Realia consists of objects from real life that are used for educational purposes. The use of realia is suppose to enhance a student's understanding of a concept. For example, using prices in a restaurant menu or clothing catalog to teach math concepts must help students learn these concepts and see their real-life applications. Regardless of the student's age or the subject matter, educators believe realia is one of most effective teaching tools. Due to the success of realia in classrooms, it is beginning to be used in the other settings. According to Kyle McCoy in the journal *History Face to Face,* museums have begun to build exhibits that allow visitors to interact with realia so that they have to develop a greater appreciation of what the museums have to offer. Museums have found that being able to interact with an authentic

object teach museum patrons and make learning much more interesting.
When people are able to use their five senses to examine an object, this
create a much greater understanding of what something is and how it works.
Although reading a book or looking at a picture may be effective in the past,
today's students and museum patrons demand to have something to hold,
use, and examine with our own hands.

CONDITIONALS, MODALS, AND NOUNS AND DETERMINERS

Edit carefully for errors in the use of conditionals, modals, and nouns and determiners. There are ten errors in the following paragraph.

The majority of fundings for education comes from two sources—the
state government and property taxes from within the school district. This
system has led to unequal funding for a rich and poor. If property taxes are
low, as they are in many inner-city and rural districts, the school funding
from these taxes would be significantly lower in poor districts than in wealthy
districts. If state governments made up for this difference, district funding
will be equal, but government funding does not do this. Government funding
is based almost entirely on the students' test scores within the districts. The
higher the test scores, the more state funding the schools receive. Only if
this situation were to create an incentive for schools to strive for better test
scores, the gap between poor and wealthy districts would disappear. In reality,
the education gap continues. Wealthier schools start with greater funding
and are able provide more teachers, smaller classrooms, better resources, a
greater variety of classes, and nicer facilities. Because all of these lead to a
better learning environment for students, they achieve higher test scores

than the students in poorer districts, and the differences in funding continue. Educators, governments, and private organizations believe that there must to be other model of funding to lessen the educational divide. However, school reform has been slow and mostly ineffective. If one of these groups should happen to design the effective model, the next challenge will be to implement it on a large scale for hundreds of poor school districts and millions of poor children.

PASSIVE VOICE, CONDITIONALS, AND SENTENCE STRUCTURE

Edit carefully for errors in the use of the passive voice, conditionals, and sentence structure. There are ten errors in the following paragraph.

Most parents of small children know that if they want their children to do something unpleasant, they would need to make it fun. For example, eating vegetables, going to bed, or doing homework. When a task is entertaining, children happily do what they are asking to do. This same theory is behind the new science of gamification, the use of games for non-game situations. Gamification produces desiring behaviors in adults by turning a tedious or negative task into a game or competition. This can see in the proliferation of competitive television shows where people lose weight, find spouses, and experience various kinds of counseling. If contestants participated in a game-like atmosphere, they are able to accomplish tasks that are impossible for them in other situations. Gamification principles have also been use to improve driver behavior on the road. While most traffic cameras snap photos of speeders who must pay traffic fines. In Sweden the cameras snap photos of drivers who are going at or under the speed limit. They are then entered in a lottery to win money that collected from speeders who have had to pay fines. By using this kind of positive reinforcement is helping solve some of the biggest problems that business and society face today.

NOUN CLAUSES, QUOTATIONS, AND CONCISE AND ACADEMIC VOCABULARY

Edit carefully for errors in the use of noun clauses and quotations. Also, concise and academic vocabulary have not been used. There are ten errors in the following paragraph.

Pamela Fletcher talks about what is it like to be a woman in American society in her essay, "Whose Body Is It, Anyway?" She compares her personal experiences as a woman to everyday incidents of women in American society. According to Fletcher, women have strengthened their status within society, yet in their relationships with men, many women still have difficulty establishing themselves as individuals or as their own person. There remains a power difference in relationships between women and individuals of the opposite sex or gender. Fletcher believes that for women to become empowered in society, they must first empower themselves, which is easier said than done. She says that women must change how they view themselves "so we can begin to see ourselves and each other as full, capable, and mighty human beings." Although this change in perspective has begun, especially women must continue to stand up for themselves and work together. Otherwise, nothing will come of passed gains and men will continue to hold all positions of power in American society. As a matter of fact, once women become empowered, they will finally be able to claim their "right to exist as whole human beings in a peaceful, humane world," according to Pamela Fletcher.

APPENDIX 1: PRACTICE WITH AUTHENTIC LANGUAGE

Chapter 1: Verb Tenses and Switching Time Frames

Read the following selection from Titan, a magazine from California State University, Fullerton. Choose the correct verb tense.

A Moveable Feast

by Laurie McLaughlin

What can an entrepreneurial spirit and a craving for a good taco get you?

For Mark Manguera, it led to launching Kogi Korean BBQ, a high-end "restaurant

on wheels"[1] that _____ $2 million its first year
          1. grossed / was grossing

and _____ a foodie phenomenon[2] throughout
      2. became / has become

Southern California since then.

    Manguera, who _____ a degree in business
          3. earned / was earning

management in 2002 followed by a degree from the California Culinary

Academy in San Francisco, envisioned the concept after a night when he

_____with friends.
4. had been clubbing / has been clubbing[3]

    "Wouldn't it be great to put Korean barbecue into a taco, put it in a truck and

park it in front of the club we just came out of?" Manguera asked a friend as they

_____ at a nearby taco truck.[4]
    5. were eating / had been eating

    In 2007, he took his idea to the streets. With $3,000 and a loaned truck, he

_____ Kogi Group with Caroline Shin and L.A.
      6. co-found / co-founded

chef Roy Choi.

....

[1] **"restaurant on wheels"** a large truck that moves from one location to another selling meals and food

[2] **foodie phenomenon** someone or something that interests people who love food and cooking

[3] **clubbing** going to night clubs

[4] **taco truck** a truck that moves from one location to another selling tacos, a Mexican dish

....

Printed with permission of Titan, The Magazine of California State University at Fullerton.

Despite doubts of friends and family, their four barbecue trucks now

_____ the Southland on any given night and
       7. dot / have dotted[5]

attract diners willing to wait hours for Korean barbecued beef in a tortilla.

The menu is a fusion of Korean and Mexican food that

_____ the multicultural roots and favorites of its
       8. reflected / reflects

creators.

It's not just the food that has earned Kogi acclaim; what currently

_____ headlines worldwide is their use of social
       9. is capturing / was capturing

media—Twitter in particular—which allows these entrepreneurs to tweet their

location, menu and schedule to more than 70,000 Twitter followers.

This marketing strategy has resulted in dozens of copycats[6] throughout the

region. "We're driven by entrepreneurial spirit,"[7] Manguera said. "That spirit

_____ to keep pushing the boundaries of our
       10. continued / will continue

industry."

....

[5] **dot** randomly cover an area with something

[6] **copycats** people who copy other people's behaviors, clothing, work, etc.

[7] **entrepreneurial spirit** attitude of a person who starts a business and takes risks to make a profit

Chapter 2: The Passive Voice and Participial Adjectives

Read the following selection from The Daily Californian, *a newspaper from the University of California, Berkeley. Choose the correct passive form.*

Study Highlights Male Bias in Animal Studies
by Claire Perlman

Research _____ on male animals,
　　　　　　1. is often only conduct / is often only conducted

even while the results _____ to men and
　　　　　　　　　　　　2. are applying / are applied

women alike, a problem University of California researchers explored in a study

_____ April 6 in the *Journal of Neuroscience.*
　　3. published / publishes

According to the study, research _____ on
　　　　　　　　　　　　4. is conducted / conducted

animals . . . does not take into account the hormonal differences between the

sexes. . . .

"Human research _____ by work in
　　　　　　5. is richly informed[1] / richly informs

animals," said co-author of the study Emily Jacobs, a postdoctoral researcher

at UC San Francisco and graduate of UC Berkeley, in an email. "But when data

from males _____ to draw conclusions about
　　　　　6. are being used / are being use

everyone's health, we risk ignoring important differences. . . ."

The study produced a result that

_____ had working memory been
7. would have been overlooked / would have overlooked

studied in only male subjects, Jacobs said. . . .

A study _____ last year by Annaliese
　　　　　8. publishes / published

Beery, a UC Berkeley graduate and current assistant professor of psychology at

Smith College, _____ a male bias[2] in eight out
　　　　　　9. found / was found

....

[1] **informed** influenced

[2] **bias** an opinion about whether a group, person, or idea is good or bad which influences how you deal with it

....

The Daily Californian, April 20, 2011. Reprinted with Permission.

of 10 of the disciplines she looked at, including neuroscience, pharmacology

and physiology.[3] The bias in neuroscience was the most evident, with 5.5 males

_____ as subjects to every female. According to
       10. used / use

Jacobs, such a bias can lead to incorrect conclusions for females, whose physiology

_____ in animal research.
  11. is often not represented / is often not representing

    Jacobs said there is bias present even in research on conditions that occur

predominantly in women, such as anxiety and multiple sclerosis, which is

"_____."
      12. alarming / alarmed

    "I suspect changes are on the horizon[4] (that) will require applicants of

federally funded research grants to justify the use of a single sex, with the

assumption that both sexes _____ by default,"[5]
      13. should now be used / should now used

Jacobs said in the email. . . .

....

[3] **physiology** the way the body of a person or animal works

[4] **on the horizon** likely to happen in the future

[5] **by default** something that is done as the usual or common way

Chapter 3: Modals

Read the following selection from The Independent, *a community newspaper from Southern California. Choose the correct modal.*

Knot Just Another Cap

by Sarah Hall

Some soft yarn and a few simple stitches _____ a

life.

                                   1. have to change / can change

Christine Shively, the founder of the charity, Knots of Love, knows that.

Her organization collects handmade knitted and crocheted[1] caps for cancer

patients going through chemotherapy.

"It's such a simple idea, but it helps in such a huge positive way," said Shively,

who started the charity in June 2007.

The organization recently launched a veteran's cap drive, the goal being to

donate 5,000 caps by Veteran's Day in November.

"I feel confident we can make it," Shively said.

"Knitters and Knotters (people who crochet) donating caps for the Veteran's

Administration[2] _____ on masculine yet soft caps

                                2. should focuses / should focus

in many different colors and sizes," Shively said.

"Veterans undergoing chemotherapy need our help and we

_____ them," Shively said.

      3. must not forget / must not to forget

    At the same time, Shively doesn't want to lessen the amount regularly

donated to other centers.

....

[1] **crocheted** made from yarn using a special needle with a hook at one end

[2] **Veteran's Administration** a government department that provides support for Americans who were in the military

....

Copyright © 2011, Firebrand Media LLC. All rights reserved. Reprinted with Permission.

Knots of Love donates to 316 facilities across the United States, Mexico, Canada and overseas. The organization has donated over 79,000 caps to date, said Shively, who has made over 3,000 caps herself. . . .

Knots of Love didn't start out so big—it was originally just a small idea.

When Shively's two sons were out of the house and she finally had some time to herself, she decided she needed a hobby.

She started making scarves and afghans[3] for friends and family. Then one of her sons asked her to make him a cap. Her first attempt was way off scale, she said.

"The first one was hysterical,"[4] Shively said. "It _____
                                       4. can have fit / could have fit
a bowling ball."

But she kept at it[5] and soon her one cap project turned into 20 caps. All her sons' friends received hats and she still made more. Soon, she began to wonder

what she _____ with all of them.
          5. could do / could have done

"I _____ a charity to donate them to,"
      6. wouldn't find /couldn't find
Shively said. "So I started my own."

What she did find was a huge need for caps at chemotherapy treatment centers. After saturating[6] the local area, Shively took the organization national.

"The charity has grown by leaps and bounds,"[7] Shively said, but volunteers are always needed. "The more knitters and crocheters we get, the more caps we

_____." . . .
      7. are able donate / can donate

....

[3] **afghans** knitted or crocheted blankets

[4] **hysterical** very funny

[5] **kept at it** continued

[6] **saturating** donating so many that there was no need for more

[7] **by leaps and bounds** increasing quickly and by a lot

Volunteer Sandy Benson has been knitting caps for Knots of Love for about

two and a half years, she said. She started just after she had retired and wanted to

do something to give back.

Benson hadn't knit in about 30 years, she said, and wasn't sure she

_____ how, so she started with a very simple cap
8. might have remembered / would remember

. . . and grew from there.

Many volunteers make one cap a week or month, Shively said. Everybody just

does what they _____. Every single cap helps, she said.
9. can do / must do

The organization asks volunteers for adult caps for both males and females.

They donate casual caps, fancy caps (often with beads or crocheted flowers), day

caps, and sleeper caps made of much softer yarn. The charity offers patterns, but

volunteers are allowed to use their own as long as[8] they use approved yarn.

"We _____ any kind of yarn," Shively
10. couldn't take / can't take

said. Chemotherapy heads are very sensitive. The wrong kind of yarn

_____ the skin and it's not comfortable."
11. may irritate / ought to irritate

A top item on Shively's wish list for the organization is UPS centers that

_____ the shipping for volunteers to send their caps
12. had better donate / will donate

to Knots of Love. It _____ much for each shipping
13. wouldn't be / must not be

center and it _____ the volunteers, she said.
14. could help really / could really help

The charity _____ monetary donations, as the
15. could use / should use

organization doesn't get a lot of money and it doesn't do a lot of fundraising.

Things always seem to work out though, Shively said, and the charity provides

an important service.

....

[8] **as long as** if

Chapter 4: Nouns and Determiners

Read the following selection from Coast Magazine, a magazine about beach life. Choose the correct nouns and determiners.

Zero Tolerance

by Steve Bramucci

Walking down the sidewalk in this new, green age,[1] it's hard not to be

surprised when you spot _____ empty bottle that never
                                 1. a / an

got recycled or a cigarette butt that escaped _____ trash.
                                                   2. the / a

No matter how _____ progress we make as eco-minded[2]
                       3. much / many

citizens, litter still seems to collect in drains and alleyways. Or it did until Chip

McDermott, _____ longtime Laguna Beach resident,
                        4. the / a

decided to do something about it. "I couldn't understand why people had come to

see _____ in the street as normal," he says. "That was my
             5. trashes / trash

call to action."[3]

    In 2007, McDermott started a street cleanup program powered by eager

citizens and local businesses . . . called ZeroTrash.org. The project is built

around "First Saturday" street cleanups, in which _____
                                                 6. the / Ø

neighbors and friends gather at businesses near their homes on

_____ first Saturday of every _____
           7. the / a   **8. months / month**

for _____ hours of urban beautification. When
            9. a little / a few

they reconvene,[4] they might go for lunch at one of ZeroTrash's sponsor

_____.
     10. restaurant / restaurants

....

[1] **green age** a time when people feel the natural environment is important

[2] **eco-minded** enthusiastic about ecology and the natural environment

[3] **call to action** event that makes a person become interested or involved

[4] **reconvene** meet again

....

Coast Magazine. Reprinted with Permission.

_____ model has been wildly successful and the
       11. A / The

results show how important ZeroTrash's efforts are. On the average First Saturday,

more than 100 _____ collect roughly 500 pounds of
       12. volunteers / volunteer

_____ from the streets. . . . This success has led to a grant[5]
    13. wastes / waste

from Miocean[6] with the aim of starting ZeroTrash chapters throughout the

county. . . .

En route to[7] collecting more than 42,000 pounds of trash from the streets,

ZeroTrash has been a force for stronger communities. McDermott understands

_____ fringe benefits[8] of his brand of grassroots activism.[9]
    14. Ø / the

"We have a Girl Scout[10] troop that helps out regularly," he says, "and some of the

high school kids have formed a club to clean up around their campus. People are

coming together, taking ownership and making a positive impact in their own

neighborhoods."

McDermott is also excited to see ZeroTrash's mission spreading. "It's

an easy model that really utilizes social networking," he says, "and all it

takes to start a thriving chapter is a lot of _____ and
       15. participation / participations

_____ energy."
  16. a few / a little

....

[5] **grant** money given to a person or a group for a particular purpose

[6] **Miocean** a nonprofit organization whose goal is to protect the coastline from pollution

[7] **En route to** On the way to

[8] **fringe benefits** additional advantages beyond what is expected

[9] **grassroots activism** actions taken by ordinary people without support from government or large organizations

[10] **Girl Scouts** an organization for girls that teaches them practical skills and helps to develop their character

For _____ eager community organizers, money

        17. a few / a little

won't be an issue. Thanks to the Miocean grant, ZeroTrash is rolling out[11] an

online contest to launch five new chapters. The winners will have their materials

purchased for them. This takes away the need for fundraising and helps get

new volunteers out on the street in _____ hurry. From

                                      18. a / the

there, McDermott hopes to see First Saturdays become a nationwide event.

"_____ People want to rely on their governments for the

       19. The / Ø

solution to _____, but I don't think that's realistic," he

         20. litters / litter

says. . . .

....

[11] **rolling out** beginning

Chapter 5: Agreement

Read the following selection from the Yale Daily News, a newspaper from Yale University. Choose the forms for correct agreement.

In Economics, Cracking the Glass Ceiling[1]

by Zoe Gorman

Earlier this year, economics professor Pinelopi Goldberg was named the first female editor in chief of the country's most prestigious economic journal, *The American Economic Review*. But Goldberg is an anomaly[2] in her field, and at Yale University. . . .

As _____ prepares to begin her duties as editor in chief in
      1. she / he
January, Goldberg, who has worked at *The American Economic Review* for the past three years, said she hopes women in economics will become more common.

" _____ a
    2. It's / Goldberg's preparation to begin her duties as editor in chief in January is
symbol of things changing," Benjamin Polak, Economics Department chair, said of Goldberg's editorial appointment. "For a long time it's been hard to encourage women to do economics."

Polak said the Economics Department is aware of

_____ gender imbalance, but he added that while
   3. the Economics Department's / its
not many junior faculty[3] _____ women until recently, now
           4. was / were
about half _____ female. Polak said the Economics Department
    5. is / are
is working hard to increase the number of tenured _____ in the
                         6. female / females

....

[1] **glass ceiling** attitudes and practices that prevent women or other groups from getting high-level jobs, even though there are no laws or rules to stop them

[2] **anomaly** something that is different from what is usual

[3] **junior faculty** faculty members that are new and less experienced

....

Copyright © 2010, Yale Daily News. Printed with Permission.

department. No faculty in the department _____ up for tenure[4]

                                         7. is / are

this year.

    Since the 2001–'02 academic year, the Economics Department has granted

tenure to only two faculty members—both men. The department now has 32

tenured male faculty, compared to three tenured female faculty. Among the 13

members of the junior faculty, however, five _____ women,

                                             8. are / is

Polak said.

    "Many of the new stars who are rising up in the profession are women," he

said. "The bad news _____ we only have three tenured women.

                        9. are / is

The good news is _____ is more than we ever had before."

               10. three tenured women / that

    Goldberg said she thinks the department is interested in promoting women

and that cases are treated fairly, but that far fewer of the candidates are female.

She added that _____ has gradually begun to

               11. this / having far fewer female candidates

change. . . .

    Goldberg proved _____ ability to juggle[5] academic and

                             12. his / her

outside responsibilities when _____ had twins 14 years ago.

                        13. Goldberg / she

Goldberg gave birth over the winter holiday, and when school started the next

week, she returned to teach.

    "I never got a break," she said. "Working with kids _____

                                          14. are / is

very difficult. You don't see _____ very much, but I think it's

                15. him or her / them

worth doing it. I think it slowed me down for a few years, but I'm glad I didn't give

up." . . .

....
[4] **tenure** the right to stay permanently in a teaching job

[5] **juggle** to fit two or more jobs or activities into your life, especially with difficulty

Still, Goldberg's rise in the field of economics has often left her among few women. Goldberg was one of only three women in her Stanford graduate school class of 22, but Goldberg said she never felt uncomfortable as a minority or faced discrimination.

"I think if I ever faced discrimination, I was totally oblivious[6] to

_____, which was a plus," she said. . . .
    16. it / discrimination

"The generation who might discriminate is gradually getting older," Polak added. "[But] I think it's still true in our society that a lot of people think that it's OK for women to be less focused on math and the science subjects. It's taken a long while to get rid of _____ convention."[7] . . .
                17. those / that

"In this day and age, I honestly think that women are empowered, and we're definitely capable of overcoming _____ biases,"[8] she said. "You
                        18. these / this
can't deny excellence." . . .

....

[6] **oblivious** unaware

[7] **convention** attitude or belief

[8] **biases** opinions about whether a group, person, or idea is good or bad, which influences how you deal with it

Chapter 6: Conditionals and Chapter 7: Sentence Structure

Read the following selection from California Educator, a magazine for teachers from kindergarten though college. Choose the forms for correct conditional sentences and sentence structure.

Math Made Cool

by Sherry Posnick-Goodwin

"I have students who have failed all their lives," says Kadhir Rajagopal,

who is also known as "Dr. Raja." "They come from poverty, broken families

_____ they have incarcerated[1] parents and other problems. But

      1. ; / ,

that doesn't mean they can't learn math."

Dr. Raja inspired a math turnaround at Grant High School in Sacramento.

His solution to students failing to understand math included developing a system

called CREATE that uses repetition to teach concepts, having students stay active

in class, immediate rewards for success, and employing tough love[2] when students

are slacking.[3]

Dr. Raja believes that learning has to happen in class. He doesn't follow

textbooks, assign homework, or spend lots of time lecturing to his students.

Without homework, . . . students are more willing to pay attention in class. If they

have trouble, he _____ them at lunch or after school.

      2. will tutor / would tutor

This young energetic teacher also succeeds by reaching students on *their* level.

He is highly interactive and uses their vocabulary. "Oh, this is a hecka bad boy," he

says to his students of an equation _____ he is writing it on the

      3. during / while

board.

....

[1] **incarcerated** in prison

[2] **tough love** a way to help someone change their behavior by being very strict but in a kind way

[3] **slacking** making little effort or being lazy in their work

....

Published with permission of the California Educator.

Mostly, Dr. Raja gives them what students of this generation crave[4]—

immediate rewards. If students _____ their hand and correctly
4. raised / raise

solve a problem in class _____ for example, 10 points are
5. , / .

immediately added to their grade. If they answer a question right on the board,

a piece of candy magically _____ on their desks. If they
6. would appear / appears

_____help, Dr. Raja is there. He flies around the classroom
7. should need / needed

at a frenetic[5] pace, lavishing[6] points, praise, rewards, and help. It's a lot of work

_____ but he knows instantly whether his students get it.[7]
8. , / ;

Mostly, they do.

To be certain his students have mastered certain concepts, every class has an

"exit" assignment _____ a math problem based on the material
9. ; / :

covered in class. If they _____ the right answer, they pass the
10. got / get

"exit" assignment. Students who don't understand the day's lesson must stay after

class or come in at lunchtime for extra help. The next step is that Dr. Raja will call

a student's parents or their coach in sports to make sure there are consequences.

Every parent is on speed-dial.[8]

"I'm a bulldog,"[9] says Dr. Raja, somewhat ferociously.

"He called my dad," agrees ninth-grader Hernan Espinosa. "He had me stay

after school so he could help me. I didn't know how to do this before, but now it's

easy for me."

[4] **crave** want

[5] **frenetic** very fast and not very organized

[6] **lavishing** giving someone or something a lot of

[7] **get it** understand

[8] **speed-dial** a special telephone feature that lets you call someone very quickly by pressing one button

[9] **bulldog** a description of a powerful person who does not give up

Chapter 7: Sentence Structure

Read the following selection from the magazine Locale, *a regional lifestyle magazine.*
Choose the correct sentence structure.

A Big Heart

by Nicky Vallee

"My mother Caterina was and is a real mom, as real as they come," says Bruno
Serato, owner of the award-winning White House Restaurant. "She raised five
boys and two girls, and was always there for us, through good times and bad. She
instilled in me the values that I carried into adulthood. Mom was always telling us
to never forget to help others and to work hard, and I haven't forgotten it." Serato
is of Italian ancestry, _____ he lived the first decade of his
       1. however / but
life in Laon, France, the city of his birth. It was there that he and the rest of the
Serato family worked as shepherds. The money was scarce, and food and clothing
were true commodities.[1] Despite these seemingly insurmountable challenges
_____ Serato says that somehow his mother always had
     2. , / .
dinner on the table and a strong example to set[2] for her children. . . .

At the age of 11, Serato moved with his family to Verona, Italy, where they
opened a small motel with a restaurant. It was there that Bruno quickly developed
a palate for unique regional cuisines[4] and became fluent in both the Italian
and French languages. Serato was called upon to wear many hats in this family
endeavor _____ chef, waiter, bartender, and maitre d'.[5]
     3. : / ;

---

[1] **commodities** valuable qualities or things

[2] **a strong example to set** was a good role model

[3] **complex** a group of buildings—*note: this word not used in this chapter.*

[4] **palate for unique regional cuisines** the ability to enjoy food from many different areas

[5] **maitre d'** someone who is in charge of a restaurant and greets guests

---

Locale Magazine. Re-birth 2011 pages 31–33. Reprinted with Permission.

"I did it all and then some," he jokes. "_____ that all
4. Little did I know / Little I knew
of this hard work was preparing me for an even greater task."

In 1975, Bruno went into the Air Force and the family sold the establishment.[6]

Four years later at age 25 and with just $200 _____ he set
5. , / .
off for the United States. Once again Serato went to work . . . as a dishwasher,

busboy, waiter, captain and maitre d'_____ this time with
6. , / .
the goal of owning his own restaurant. Sure enough, the opportunity to buy The

White House Restaurant arrived in 1987. . . .

"It wasn't easy, and I was working 17 hours a day," he recalls. "I slept at The

White House more than one night because I was doing everything. . . ."

Under Serato's reign, the establishment became one of the most renowned

and popular dining establishments, and he may have been satisfied

_____ at that point to live out his working days in the
7. Ø / .
earned comfort of success. That wasn't to be the case.[7] In 2005, Serato heard

that the Boys and Girls Club[8] of Anaheim was facing serious challenges to their

fundraising efforts.

"They weren't doing well at all," he says. "That's _____
8. when did I hear / when I heard
about the large number of children who were living in motels with their families.

Most of them were not able to afford dinner . . . I knew I had to do something."

He cooked up some pasta right on the spot[9] and delivered it to the Club.

That was on April 18, 2005. Since that day, Serato has served a quarter of a million

meals to disadvantaged children. That first night, he dished out food for at least

....
[6] **establishment** business

[7] **That wasn't to be the case** That was not going to happen

[8] **Boys and Girls Club** an organization for young people in the U.S. that arranges activities and gives help with problems

[9] **on the spot** at the exact moment and location

100 kids. Since then the numbers have grown to nearly 200 meals every night of

the week. Now, the restaurant owner once known for dishing out culinary works of

art to his discerning[10] customers _____ is referred to by his

9. he / Ø

adoring pint-sized fan base[11] as "The Pasta Man.". . .

While Serato admits that his bottom line[12] has suffered due to the scale of the

effort _____ he believes that making people aware of the

10. , /.

issue facing the children he serves is of greater importance. . . .

"I feel like I'm saying thank you," Serato says, his voice cracking a bit. "Mom

told us to never take anything from anyone as if we were entitled to it.[13] The man

I am today is _____ her. My house is always open to people

11. because / because of

because of her."

From the looks of the pasta line that forms like clockwork[14] each night at the

Boys and Girls Club, so is his heart.

....

[10] **discerning** able to make good judgments

[11] **pint-sized fan base** a group of children who admire someone or something

[12] **bottom line** profit or amount of money a business earns or loses

[13] **as if we were entitled to it** as if we had the right to it

[14] **clockwork** happening at the same time and in the same way every time

Chapter 8: Noun Clauses and Using Sources

Read the following selection from Parade's Healthy Style, a Sunday newspaper magazine on nutrition, fitness, and health-related news. Choose the correct form and use of noun clauses and quotations.

The Rise of Hypochondria
by Lynn Schnurnberger

For tens of thousands of Americans who suffer from hypochondria, every headache is a brain tumor and a simple cold spells cancer.

"Hypochondriacs have an overwhelming belief that any symptom,[1] no matter how innocuous,[2] will lead to a serious disease _____"

                     1. , / Ø

says Dr. Arthur Barsky, a professor of psychiatry at Harvard, who says

_____ an estimated 5% to 12% of patients who see doctors every

    2. that / what

year are hypochondriacs. The Internet hasn't helped. Hundreds of medical sites have produced a new strain of hypochondria called "cyberchondria."

The problem has grown to such disturbing proportions[3] that the National Institutes of Health has funded a five-year study to compare the efficacy of treatments.[4] People who suffer from hypochondria can't focus on anything else. Many lose their jobs and their relationships, believes Jane Pearson, Ph.D., of the National Institute of Mental Health. The NIH hopes _____ the

                                     3. how / Ø

results will reduce what experts estimate to be billions of dollars that are spent every year on unnecessary tests and doctor visits.

....

[1] **symptom** a sign that an illness exists

[2] **innocuous** not dangerous or harmful

[3] **to such disturbing proportions** so large

[4] **the efficacy of treatments** how effective different treatments are

March/April 2010 © 2010 Lynn Schnurnberger. Initially published in Parade's Healthy Style. All rights reserved. Printed with Permission.

Could This Be You?

Anyone can develop hypochondria. A childhood illness or death of a loved one

can trigger[5] it, and medical professionals are often prone.[6] The difference between

a hypochondriac and someone with reasonable health concerns is their "degree of

reassurability," _____ says. "When test results are negative, most people

             4. Arthur / Dr. Barsky

believe their doctor. But the hypochondriac can't be reassured."

"If you manage to convince a hypochondriac that he doesn't have an ulcer, two

days later he'll come back complaining _____ that he's suffering from

                  5. , / Ø

Parkinson's disease,"[7] says James Pennebaker, chair of the psychology department at the

University of Texas at Austin.

    Jennifer Traig, 39, _____

        6. Ø / the author of *Well Enough Alone: A Cultural History of My Hypochondria,*

remembers that in grammar school she _____ about losing her eyesight

                7. worries / worried

and later became convinced she had multiple sclerosis,[8] though tests ruled it out. "I felt

like I was going crazy," says Traig, who is now symptom-free thanks to a regimen of Prozac

and cognitive therapy.[9]

New Treatments

It is possible to disrupt a hypochondriac's fixation.[10] Harvard's Dr. Barsky uses

cognitive therapy to teach patients how to counter[11] panicky thoughts. "If a patient has

[5] **trigger** to make something happen very quickly

[6] **prone** likely to do something, especially something harmful

[7] **Parkinson's disease** a disease of the central nervous system

[8] **multiple sclerosis** a disease that destroys a person's nerves

[9] **cognitive therapy** a type of psychological counseling

[10] **fixation** overly strong interest in something or obsession

[11] **counter** reduce the bad effects of

a backache, I ask _____ besides a tumor. Perhaps

9. what it could be / what could it be

he lifted something the wrong way. Writing down alternative scenarios can be

calming. If someone complains of a swollen lymph node,[12] I'll tell him he can't

keep poking it, because that will make it more tender, which will convince the

patient that it is getting worse. I'll limit him to examining it twice a day and then

once, and often, the problem will go away. The idea is to create a delay between

the patient's impulse to obsess and examine himself."

Studies by Dr. Brian Fallon, a professor of Clinical Psychiatry at Columbia

University, show that drugs _____ reduce symptoms within

10. help / helped

12 weeks. "Both cognitive therapy and medication are effective, but which

treatment—or combination of treatments—is better _____

11. remain / remains

to be seen," Dr. Fallon says. In the meantime, a turn of phrase[13] may make all

the difference. "Nobody likes to be called a hypochondriac. It has such negative

connotations," he says. Which is _____

12. why his patients have / why do his patients have

"Heightened Illness Concern."

....

[12] **lymph node** a small gland in the body

[13] **a turn of phrase** saying something in a different way

Chapter 9: Conciseness/Brevity

Read the following selection from California Educator, a magazine for teachers from kindergarten though college. Choose the most concise form.

Should Schools Be More Consistent in Grading Students?

by Sherry Posnick-Goodwin

Some universities, _____ Stanford Law

1. which include / including

School, Yale University, and UC Berkeley's Boalt Hall School of Law, have dropped

letter grades and shifted to other forms of evaluation, such as "honors," "pass,"

"restricted credit," or "no credit." The goal is to eliminate students from "class

shopping," or choosing teachers _____ for being

2. known / who are known

easier on grading. _____ some schools, like the

3. Conversely / On the other hand

University of California, Santa Cruz, have abandoned the "pass/fail" system and

brought back traditional grades.

The *Los Angeles Times* recently reported that Douglas Reeves,

_____, conducted

4. who is an expert on grading systems / an expert on grading systems

an experiment that demonstrated how subjective grading can be. He

asked more than 10,000 educators in the United States, Australia, Canada,

and South America to determine a final semester grade for a student

_____ the following grades for assignments

5. who received / receiving

in this order: C, C, MA (missing assignment), D, C, B, MA, MA, B, and A. The

educators _____ gave the hypothetical[2] student

6. surveyed[1] / who were surveyed

final grades ranging from A to F because they used different criteria[3] for grading.

....

[1] **surveyed** questioned

[2] **hypothetical** not real; imagined

[3] **criteria** standards

....

"Making the grade" by Sherry Posnick-Goodwin. Published with permission of the California Educator.

Getting educators on the "same page"[4] with grades is challenging but

_____, says Jessica Breed, a 10th grade
7. possible / it is possible

English teacher at Beaumont High School, where department members

_____ decided that teachers should all grade on the
8. jointly / jointly together

same criteria.

"There were big differences among teachers on how many points timed essays were

worth, how much homework was worth, and whether late work should be accepted,"

says Breed. "Some teachers were accepting late work until the final day of the semester

and some wouldn't accept work _____.
9. that was even an hour overdue / even an hour overdue

After lots of meetings, a uniform[5] grading policy was implemented[6] for English

and math teachers. In the English Department, for example, teachers decided major

assignments were worth 90 percent of earned credit the first day late and 50 percent of

earned credit the next four days.

"I think it's fair when teachers grade the same way," says 10th grader Kaitlyn Nelson.

"Nobody has _____ this
10. a teacher who is easier or a teacher who is harder / easier or harder teachers

way and everybody knows what to expect."

Breed says teachers are more empowered when they are unified.

_____, she doesn't foresee a universal grading system
11. But nevertheless / Nevertheless

happening across the _____ state anytime soon.
12. whole / whole entire

"It was such an effort just getting 15 people to compromise in our department," she

says. "I can't imagine getting agreement on a consistent grading policy statewide."

....

[4] **on the "same page"** working together and having the same goals

[5] **uniform** the same in all ways and with all members

[6] **implemented** started

Chapter 10: Academic Vocabulary

Read the following selection from The Hornet, *the student newspaper from Fullerton College. Choose the academic vocabulary.*

Students Donate the Gift of Life
by Krysta Fauria

The Associated Students[1] _____ a blood drive

               1. was responsible for / sponsored

with the help of the Red Cross on Wednesday and Thursday in the Student Center.

Lisa Tseng, the Red Cross member _____ the

              2. in charge of / leading

blood drive, expressed her belief that if more people knew every donation of blood

was used _____, more people would donate.

      3. immediately / right away

Members of the Red Cross who _____

          4. participated in / took part in

the blood drive said that _____ citizens

      5. lots of / many

_____ the need for blood in the United States.

6. don't know about / are unaware of

"Every two seconds a bag of blood is needed in the United States," stated

Tseng.

Many students volunteered to donate for the first time, saying the

gratification[2] of helping someone made the experience worthwhile.

"It was my first time giving blood. I have always wanted to donate but never

had the opportunity to sign up," reported blood donor Alex Shaffer. "I think it's a

rewarding _____, knowing that you are helping

      7. experience / thing to do

save lives."

....

[1] Associated Students a group of student leaders at a college or university

[2] gratification satisfaction

....

The Hornet, October 20, 2010. Volume 96 Issue 8. Reprinted with Permission.

The number of people giving blood would probably

_____ if they knew how high the demand for
8. increase / go up

blood was. . . .

In addition to giving blood, students were also encouraged to

_____ for the National Marrow Donor Program.
9. register / sign up

Leukemia patients and those suffering from other blood related diseases often

need bone marrow[3] to survive.

Because it is more difficult to find a match for a marrow transplant, Be A

Hero Become A Donor, or BAHBAD, encourages everyone to sign up for the bone

marrow registry.

BAHBAD is an organization that supports blood donation and participation

in the marrow registry. . . . Gina Cousineau, the executive director of BAHBAD,

_____ how her son's need for bone marrow
10. talked about / explained

inspired her to become educated and to help the cause.

"Who better to educate and empower than people who already understand

the importance of saving lives?" Cousineau asked.

....
[3] **bone marrow** a soft substance in the empty centers of bones that produces blood cells

APPENDIX 2: IRREGULAR VERBS

Base Form	Simple Past	Past Participle	Base Form	Simple Past	Past Participle
awake	awoke	awoken	find	found	found
be	was, were	been	fit	fit	fit
beat	beat	beaten/beat	flee	fled	fled
become	became	become	fly	flew	flown
begin	began	begun	forbid	forbade	forbidden
bend	bent	bent	forecast	forecast	forecast
bet	bet	bet	forget	forgot	forgotten
bind	bound	bound	forgive	forgave	forgiven
bite	bit	bitten	freeze	froze	frozen
bleed	bled	bled	get	got	gotten/got
blow	blew	blown	give	gave	given
break	broke	broken	go	went	gone
bring	brought	brought	grind	ground	ground
broadcast	broadcast	broadcast	grow	grew	grown
build	built	built	hang	hung	hung
burn	burned	burned	have	had	had
buy	bought	bought	hear	heard	heard
catch	caught	caught	hide	hid	hidden
choose	chose	chosen	hit	hit	hit
cling	clung	clung	hold	held	held
come	came	come	hurt	hurt	hurt
cost	cost	cost	keep	kept	kept
creep	crept	crept	know	knew	known
cut	cut	cut	lay	laid	laid
deal	dealt	dealt	lead	led	led
dig	dug	dug	leave	left	left
dive	dove	dived	lend	lent	lent
do	did	done	let	let	let
draw	drew	drawn	lie	lay	lain
dream	dreamed/dreamt	dreamed/dreamt	light	lit/lighted	lit/lighted
drink	drank	drunk	lose	lost	lost
drive	drove	driven	make	made	made
eat	ate	eaten	mean	meant	meant
fall	fell	fallen	meet	met	met
feed	fed	fed	mislead	misled	misled
feel	felt	felt	mistake	mistook	mistaken
fight	fought	fought	misunderstand	misunderstood	misunderstood

Base Form	Simple Past	Past Participle	Base Form	Simple Past	Past Participle
overcome	overcame	overcome	spread	spread	spread
pay	paid	paid	spring	sprang	sprung
prove	proved	proven/proved	stand	stood	stood
put	put	put	steal	stole	stolen
quit	quit	quit	stick	stuck	stuck
read	read	read	sting	stung	stung
rid	rid	rid	stink	stank/stunk	stunk
ride	rode	ridden	strike	struck	struck/stricken
ring	rang	rung	string	strung	strung
rise	rose	risen	strive	strove/strived	striven
run	ran	run	swear	swore	sworn
say	said	said	sweep	swept	swept
see	saw	seen	swim	swam	swum
seek	sought	sought	swing	swung	swung
sell	sold	sold	take	took	taken
send	sent	sent	teach	taught	taught
set	set	set	tear	tore	torn
sew	sewed	sewn/sewed	tell	told	told
shake	shook	shaken	think	thought	thought
shed	shed	shed	throw	threw	thrown
shine	shone/shined	shone/shined	understand	understood	understood
shoot	shot	shot	undertake	undertook	undertaken
show	showed	shown	undo	undid	undone
shrink	shrank/shrunk	shrunk/shrunken	uphold	upheld	upheld
shut	shut	shut	upset	upset	upset
sing	sang	sung	wake	woke	woken/waked
sit	sat	sat	wear	wore	worn
sleep	slept	slept	weave	wove	woven
slide	slid	slid	weep	wept	wept
speak	spoke	spoken	wet	wet	wet
speed	sped/speeded	sped/speeded	win	won	won
spend	spent	spent	wind	wound	wound
spin	spun	spun	withdraw	withdrew	withdrawn
spit	spit/spat	spat	write	wrote	written
split	split	split			

APPENDIX 3: COMPARATIVES AND SUPERLATIVES

Use this appendix to review comparative and superlative forms.

Comparatives of Adjectives and Adverbs

Use comparatives when you are looking at the similarities between two related things.

1. Add the comparative suffix *–er* to one-syllable adjectives and adverbs. Since *–er* means "more (than)," do not use *more* with a word that has an *–er* suffix.

    *Good athletes are generally tall**er** than the average person.* (adjective)

    not

    Good athletes are generally more taller than the average person.

    *Good students work hard**er** than poor students.* (adverb)

    not

    Good students work more harder than poor students.

2. For most adjectives and adverbs with two or more syllables, use *more* for comparatives.

    *Springtime in the desert is beautiful, but it's **more beautiful** in the mountain high country.* (adjective)

    *Engineers must design buildings carefully, but construction workers must implement the designs **more carefully**.* (adverb)

3. Use *less* with most adjectives and adverbs when making comparisons.

    *During the winter, car dealerships are **less busy** than in the summertime.*

    *Poor students work **less carefully** than good students.*

4. Some adjectives and adverbs have irregular comparative forms.

    Better is the comparative form of the adjective *good* and the adverb *well*.

    *Jose is a **good** student.   Jose is a **better** student than Paula.* (adjective)

    *Maria sings **well**.   Maria sings **better** than Lee.* (adverb)

    Worse is the comparative form of the adjective *bad* and the adverb *badly*.

    *Many people have **bad** spelling in English.   Some adults have **worse** spelling than children have.* (adjective)

    *Beginning drivers drive **badly**.   Some experienced drivers drive **worse** than beginning drivers.* (adverb)

    Note: Include *than* if stating the second half of the comparison; however, it is not always necessary to mention the second half. You may also include the verb or its auxiliary.

    *Short distance runners are faster __than__ **long distance runners (are)**.*

    *Speed walkers walk faster __than__ **most people (do)**.*

Superlatives of Adjectives and Adverbs

Use superlatives when you are comparing three or more things and stating that one of them has the highest degree of the group.

1. Add the superlative suffix *–est* to one-syllable adjectives and adverbs. Include *the* before the adjective or adverb. Since *–est* means "the most," do not use *the most* with a word that has an *–est* suffix.

    *Vatican City is **the smallest** country in Europe.* (adjective)

    not

    Vatican City is the most smallest country in Europe.

    *The Bugatti Veyron finished **the fastest** in a car race.* (adverb)

    not

    The Bugatti Veyron finished the most fastest in a car race.

2. For most adjectives and adverbs with two syllables or more, use *the most*.

   *Library databases are **the most convenient** method to do research.*

   *The numbers 7, 5, 2, 1, and 3 occur **the most frequently** in winning lottery tickets.*

3. Some adjectives and adverbs have irregular superlative forms.

   Best is the superlative form of the adjective *good* and the adverb *well*.

   *Many people believe that Shakespeare's "Othello" is a **good** tragedy but that "Hamlet" is his **best** tragedy.* (adjective)

   *Students learn to write **well** in school, but it's not until they reach the workplace that they learn to write **the best** for their field.* (adverb)

   Worst is the superlative form of the adjective *bad* and the adverb *badly*.

   *Many kinds of diets are unhealthy, but liquid diets are **the worst** method to lose weight.* (adjective)

   *Statistics show that people drive **the worst** on July 4 as large numbers of accidents happen on this day.* (adverb)

4. Use *the least* with most adjectives and adverbs.

   *January is **the least busy** time of the year for retail stores.*

   *Blood type AB negative occurs **the least frequently** of all blood types.*

5. The superlative adjective or adverb is often followed by a noun and/or prepositional phrase, which indicates what is being compared.

   *Soap operas have been **the most popular** <u>daytime television shows</u> for decades.*

   *The names Jacob and Emily were **the most popular** <u>between 2000 and 2009</u> in the United States.*

APPENDIX 4: VERB FORMS

Use this appendix to review some of the rules about verb form in English. There are five basic verb forms that you should be familiar with.

Base Form	give
Third-Person Singular	gives
Simple Past	gave
Present Participle (*-ing* form)	giving
Past Participle (form ending in *-ed / -en / -t*)	given

These verb forms are used in the following ways.

The Simple Tenses

In the simple present, use the base form and third-person singular. Use the auxiliary verb *do* in negatives and questions except with the verb *be*. (See Chapter 1.)

*The library **opens** at 9:00 A.M.*

*The on-line services usually **operate** 24 hours a day.*

*Vegans **do not eat** any animal products.*

*Why **do** vegans **reject** the use of animal products?*

*The Harvest Moon **is** in late September.*

*A Blue Moon **is not** an annual occurrence.*

In the simple past, use the simple past form of the verb. Use the auxiliary verb *did* in negatives and questions except with the verb *be*. (See Chapter 1.)

*The first satellite **visited** the moon in 1957.*

*Bell bottom pants **went** out of style in the 1970s.*

*The storm **did not produce** flooding.*

*What **did** the research **teach** us?*

*The old immigration law **was** illegal.*

*The Congress **was not** in session yesterday.*

Note: The auxiliary verb *do* is always followed by the base form of the verb.

*They **did not come**.*

They did not ~~came~~. not

The Progressive Tenses

In the present progressive and past progressive, use the auxiliary *be* followed by the present participle of the main verb (*-ing* form). The form of *be* shows the present or past time. (See Chapter 1.)

***Are** the rebels **taking over** the current government?* (present progressive)

*Last year at this time, the federal government **was working on** healthcare reform.* (past progressive)

The Perfect Tenses

In the present perfect and past perfect, use the auxiliary *have* followed by the past participle of the main verb (form ending in *–ed, -en,* or *-t*). The form of *have* shows the present or past time. (See Chapter 1.)

***Has** the economy **recovered** from the recession yet?* (present perfect)

*The first recession **had ended** by the final years of the decade.* (past perfect)

Modals

In the present or future, modals are always followed by the base form of the main verb. (See Chapter 3.)

Students **should review** their notes before class begins.

Can new technology **help** clean up the environment?

In the past, modals are usually followed by *have* and the past participle of the main verb (form ending in *–ed, -en,* or *-t*).

The first humans may have existed over four million years ago.

Should the researchers **have published** their findings sooner?

Gerunds and Infinitives

In addition to the five basic forms, English verbs also have a gerund (verb + *-ing*) and an infinitive form (*to* + verb). In these forms, however, the verb no longer acts as a verb. Gerunds and infinitives act as nouns—for example, as subjects or as objects of verbs and prepositions.

Verb + Gerund or Infinitive

Some verbs are followed by either a gerund or an infinitive as their object. These verbs include: *begin, continue, hate, like, love, prefer,* and *start*.

Most children **love being / to be** with their parents until the children reach puberty.

Verb + Gerund

Some verbs are followed by a gerund but not an infinitive as their object. These verbs include: *appreciate, avoid, consider, delay, discuss, dislike, enjoy, finish, keep, mention, mind, miss, quit,* and *suggest*.

Athletes **avoid exercising** outside if the temperature is over 90 degrees.

Verb + Infinitive

Some verbs are followed by an infinitive but not a gerund as their object. These verbs include: *agree, ask, decide, expect, hope, intend, learn, offer, plan, pretend, seem,* and *want*.

The professor **agreed to give** extra credit last semester.

Some verbs are followed by a noun + infinitive. These verbs include: *advise, ask, encourage, expect, force, invite, order, remind, tell, warn,* and *want*.

They **invited us to visit** them in their new home.

Preposition + Gerund

Prepositions such as *in, on, by, for,* and *with* can be followed by gerunds but not infinitives.

The student gave an unacceptable reason **for submitting** late work.

Phrasal verbs and other verb + preposition combinations can also be followed by gerunds but not infinitives.

The president **put off signing** the bill until after the election.

The elderly **are accustomed to living** by themselves.

Common phrasal verbs include: *apologize for, believe in, complain about, give up, insist on, keep on, look forward to, plan on, put off, take care of, talk about,* and *think about*.

Common *be* + adjective + preposition combinations followed by gerunds include: *be accustomed to, be afraid of, be bored with, be excited about, be interested in, be preoccupied with, be tired of,* and *be worried about*.

Verb + Base Form

The verbs *make, have, let,* and *help* can mean to cause someone to do something or to allow someone to do something. When they are used in this way, these verbs are followed by the base form of a verb. *Make, have, let,* and *help* must be followed by a pronoun or noun phrase + the base form of the verb. *Help* can be followed by an infinitive instead of a base form.

*The firefighters **made the residents leave** their homes, and they **had them go** to shelters in the next city.*

*Many parents **let their children drive** at sixteen years old.*

*Can your congressional representative **help you change** the law?*

APPENDIX 5: WORD FORMS

Use this appendix to review the word forms in English. Some basic word forms include:

Verb	Good students **succeed** because they work hard.
Noun	Everyone has a different definition of **success**.
Adjective	Some people are **successful** because of luck and timing.
Adverb	When people **successfully** complete an activity, they feel good about themselves.

The suffix, or ending, of a word can help you recognize its part of speech.

Verb Suffixes

Common verb suffixes include:

-ate	investigate
-en	lengthen
-ify	notify
-ize	familiarize

Noun Suffixes

Common noun suffixes include:

-ance	tolerance
-cy	accuracy
-ence	difference
-er	writer
-ion	permission
-ism	socialism
-ist	communist
-ity	possibility
-ment	involvement
-ness	happiness
-or	actor
-ship	friendship

Adverb Suffixes

There is only one common adverb suffix.

-ly	happily

Adjective Suffixes

Common adjective suffixes include:

-able	acceptable
-al	classical
-an/-ian	African, Floridian
-ant	tolerant
-ate	literate
-ed	excited
-ent	dependent
-ese	Chinese
-ful	helpful
-ible	responsible
-ic	allergic
-ing	boring
-ish	foolish
-ive	creative
-less	careless
-like	childlike
-ly	friendly
-ous	famous
-some	handsome
-y	scary

Adjective Suffixes –ed and –ing

The adjective suffix *–ing* means "causing a feeling." The adjective suffix *–ed* means "experiencing a feeling." The *–ed* adjectives are often used to describe people, whereas the *–ing* adjectives are often used to describe things and actions as well as people.

*It was a **boring** movie, so the audience felt very **bored**.* (boring = causing a feeling; bored = experiencing a feeling)

*At the end of the **tiring** exam, the **tired** students were happy to have a vacation.* (tiring = causing a feeling; tired = experiencing a feeling)

APPENDIX 6: CONCISE WORD LIST

WORDY	CONCISE
advance planning	planning
all of a sudden	suddenly
an unexpected surprise	a surprise
as a matter of fact	in fact
ask a question	ask
at a later date	later
at the present time	now
at the same time	simultaneously
a total of twenty	twenty
basic fundamentals	fundamentals
be able to	can
be in need of	need
but nevertheless	but *or* nevertheless
combine/connect/mix together	combine/connect/mix
completely full	full
dangerous weapon	weapon
divide up	divide
during the time that	while
each and every	each *or* every
end result	result
first/last of all	first/last
fewer in number	fewer
for the reason that	because
good benefit	benefit
green in color	green
in every instance	always
in my opinion I think	in my opinion *or* I think
in order to	to
in spite of the fact that	in spite of *or* although
in the event that	if
in the near future	soon
in this day and age	today
just exactly	exactly
a large number of	many
might possibly	might *or* possibly
new innovation	innovation
on a regular basis	regularly
on the other hand	conversely
past history	history
postpone until later	postpone
refer back	refer
repeat again	repeat
return back	return
serious crisis	crisis
small in size	small
square in shape	square
sufficient enough	sufficient *or* enough
ten in number	ten
three different kinds	three kinds
up above	above
very unique	unique
write down	write

APPENDIX 7: ACADEMIC WORD LIST

The Academic Word List was developed in 2000 by Averil Coxhead from written material used in the fields of liberal arts, commerce, law, and science. It contains 570 words that appear most frequently in this material.

Chapter 1
academic
adults
assign
assigned
available
aware
capability
concluded
conducting
contrast
correspond
culture
decade
define
documents
energy
established
eventually
exposure
facilities
feature
focus
foundation
founded
generations
goal
grade
illegal
incidents
integration
journals
layer
locating
negative
negative
norm
occurs
positive
preliminary
previous
published
recreated

relax
release
requirements
research
researchers
residential
similar
site
sought
stress
supplement
theory
transformed
transforming
widespread

Chapter 2
achieve
achieved
affecting
areas
assume
challenged
challenging
commissioned
compensate
convinced
create
creativity
culture
discriminate
document
environment
eventually
expert
featured
federal
funded
funding
hierarchy
ignored
immigrants
job
label

legal
locate
located
professional
prospect
psychology
removal
role
substitute
theory
tracing
visibility

Chapter 3
access
amendment
approximately
areas
assumed
author
constitutional
consumers
controversial
created
denied
depressed
document
economic
emerged
emerging
established
evidence
financial
focuses
granted
immigrants
immigration
job
legal
locate
location
logic
maintain
medical

nevertheless
outcome
period
primarily
proceedings
region
registers
respond
responded
restriction
revolution
significantly
technological
traditional

Chapter 4
academic
affect
alter
approach
concentration
dominate
economically
emerging
errors
files
globe
hierarchical
hierarchies
hypothesis
input
instructions
intelligence
involved
medical
method
military
motivation
negative
normally
obvious
positive
previous
priority

research
researchers
residents
response
restrictions
revolution
revolutionary
similar
structure
submit
targets
text
trigger
underlying
unique

Chapter 5

accompany
areas
assist
benefit
benefits
capability
communities
computers
consequences
contact
convinced
creations
decline
diminished
economic
economically
environment
equipment
estimated
ethical
ethics
eventually
evidence
exposed
financial
incidence
inserted
isolation
location
majority
medical
mental

methods
negative
overall
participate
physical
positive
procedures
promote
recovery
require
research
roles
stable
style
tasks
theory
virtual
volunteer
volunteering
volunteers

Chapter 6

access
achieving
adapt
adjust
adult
approximately
area
aspects
attachments
bond
bonds
circumstances
consulting
contracts
created
creating
creative
culture
despite
dramatically
editing
emerged
environment
equipment
exposed
funding
insecure

issue
job
legislators
legislature
major
majority
mature
minority
nevertheless
normal
occurred
occurs
options
period
physical
physically
predictable
professional
ranges
release
resources
scenarios
schedule
secure
seek
significantly
similar
specifically
style
unique
vision
volumes

Chapter 7

access
achievement
administrative
adult
assignment
chapter
clarified
communities
computer
constant
controversy
deny
detect
devices
devote

disposal
economic
elements
established
evaluated
experts
format
founded
goal
identify
innovations
intelligent
involvement
located
logical
majority
mental
physical
principles
process
promote
publisher
purchase
pursuing
research
revolution
status
structure
technology
thesis
topic
ultimate
ultimately

Chapter 8

academics
accompanied
adults
appreciation
appropriate
assistant
author
available
challenging
community
culture
debate
decades
depressed

dynamic
environment
established
finally
focus
focused
founder
generation
goal
guarantee
ignore
immigrant
indicate
inevitable
initially
investment
involves
maintain
mature
maturity
military
negative
physical
previous
primary
psychologists
psychology
relaxation
release
remove
respond
response
reveal
seeking
similar
stress
stressed
stressful
symbol
tasks
techniques
temporarily
tradition
traditional
transferring
ultimate
unique

Chapter 9
achieved
administrators
affected
areas
aspects
awareness
beneficial
benefits
chemicals
clarity
construction
credit
definitely
definition
design
economic
economically
eliminate
energy
enhances
environment
finally
foundation
furthermore
generations
individual
involved
job
label
liberator
located
mental
military
nevertheless
participating
participation
perspective
physical
psychology
recover
regional
release
research
researchers
revolution
revolutionary
revolutions

specific
topic
unified
variations
version

Chapter 10
accurately
affected
area
aspect
capability
complex
consequences
consumption
create
culture
debate
decades
designer
diverse
eliminate
eliminated
emerged
energy
environments
established
experts
facility
factors
feature
focus
focusing
function
grants
impact
incapable
inserting
involved
locations
maintains
major
medical
methods
migrate
nuclear
occurs
outcome

participating
percent
physical
procedure
promoted
ranges
reactor
regions
registered
released
rely
research
role
shift
source
techniques
traditional
unique
unstable

Chapter 11
achieve
adults
advocates
appreciation
approximately
beneficial
capable
cease
challenge
chemicals
coincide
communication
computer
concept
consists
create
culture
define
design
devices
eliminating
enhance
environment
establish
establishing
eventually
evidence

Appendix 1

institute
jobs
medical
mental
negative
professionals
psychology
research
scenarios
sites
trigger

Chapter 9
abandoned
challenging
consistent
conversely
credit
criteria
demonstrated
eliminate
evaluation
expert
final

goal
grade
grading
hypothetical
implemented
major
nevertheless
percent
policy
ranging
restricted
shifted

surveyed
traditional
unified
uniform

Chapter 10
participated
participation
register
survive
unaware
volunteered

APPENDIX 8: CORRECTION SYMBOLS

Your teacher may use symbols to indicate specific error types in your writing. The charts below include symbols, explanations, and sample sentences for some of these errors. You can use these symbols to help make the necessary corrections while editing your own work. Chart 1 refers to grammar topics that are presented in *Grammar for Writing 3*. For further explanation and practice, refer to the appropriate chapters or appendices. Chart 2 presents other common correction symbols.

CHART 1

SYMBOL	MEANING	SAMPLE SENTENCE	*GRAMMAR FOR WRITING 3*
cs	comma splice (using a comma to connect two sentences)	cs It was a beautiful day, there wasn't a cloud in the sky.	Chapter 7
det	determiner error	det It is a most interesting book that I have read.	Chapter 4
frag	fragment (a partial sentence punctuated as a complete sentence)	frag When we practice. The team must work together.	Chapter 7
id	problem with idioms or set expressions	id We always agree to our teachers.	Chapters 9, 10
num	noun error (number)	num We have enough homeworks to last a week.	Chapter 4
p	punctuation error	p I remember, graduation as the most memorable event.	Chapters 6, 7, 8
ro	run on (two or more sentences without punctuation between them)	ro The lecture was very interesting it went by so fast.	Chapter 7
s-v	subject-verb agreement	s-v She never go to the library to study.	Chapter 5
t	verb tense error	t We haven't completed the project yesterday.	Chapter 1
vb	verb form error	vb They haven't went to the gym in weeks.	Chapters 1, 2, 3, 6 Appendix 4
wf	word form error	wf Her father is the most success software engineer in the firm.	Appendix 5
//	faulty parallelism	// We hoped for relaxation, peace and to have good weather.	Chapter 7

CHART 2

SYMBOL	MEANING	SAMPLE SENTENCE
sp	spelling error	sp My apartment is <u>noisey</u> and expensive.
ww	wrong word	ww He is the best offensive player <u>in</u> the team.
^	insert missing word	in They are interested ^ going with us to the concert.
℘	delete	His writing is clear, and concise, and interesting to read.
¶	paragraph	This is the main theme. ¶ A secondary theme explains . . .
#	add a space	# My friends went to the club even^though it's very expensive.
⟲→	move here	The essay was interesting that we stayed up all night writing.
⌐	transpose	We hardly could remember the way to your house.

APPENDIX 9: EDITING LOG

Use this editing log or create a similar one of your own to keep track of the grammar errors that you make in your writing. By logging and correcting your errors, you will begin to see which errors you make the most frequently. Once you recognize the grammar topics that are the most problematic for you, editing becomes easier.

ERROR	SYMBOL	ORIGINAL SENTENCE	REVISED SENTENCE
Parallel Structure	//	My father's strength, wisdom, and determine have influenced my life.	My father's strength, wisdom, and <u>determination</u> have influenced my life.

APPENDIX 10: GRAMMAR BOOK REFERENCES

GRAMMAR FOR WRITING 3	UNDERSTANDING AND USING ENGLISH GRAMMAR, FOURTH EDITION	FOCUS ON GRAMMAR 5, FOURTH EDITION
Chapter 1 Expressing Present, Past, and Future; Switching Time Frames	Chapter 1 Overview of the Verb Tenses Chapter 2 Present and Past; Simple and Progressive Chapter 3 Perfect and Perfect Progressive Tenses Chapter 4 Future Time Chapter 5 Review of Verb Tenses Chapter 6 Subject-Verb Agreement: 6–2	Unit 1 Present Time Unit 2 Past Time Unit 3 Future Time
Chapter 2 The Passive Voice and Participial Adjectives	Chapter 11 The Passive Chapter 15 Gerunds and Infinitives, Part 2: 15–4, 15–5, 15–8	Unit 9 Modifications of Nouns Unit 14 The Passive: Review and Expansion Unit 15 The Passive to Describe Situations and to Report Opinions
Chapter 3 Modals	Chapter 9 Modals, Part 1 Chapter 10 Modals, Part 2	Unit 4 Modals to Express Degrees of Necessity Unit 5 Modals to Express Degrees of Certainty
Chapter 4 Nouns and Determiners	Chapter 7 Nouns	Unit 6 Count and Non-Count Nouns Unit 7 Definite and Indefinite Articles Unit 8 Quantifiers
Chapter 5 Agreement	Chapter 6 Subject-Verb Agreement Chapter 8 Pronouns: 8–2, 8–3, 8–5	Part III From Grammar to Writing: Agreement
Chapter 6 Conditionals	Chapter 17 Adverb Clauses: 17–6, 17–7, 17–8, 17–9, 17–10, 17–11 Chapter 20 Conditional Sentences and Wishes	Unit 22 Conditionals; Other Ways to Express Unreality Unit 23 More Conditions; The Subjunctive
Chapter 7 Sentence Structure and Word Order	Chapter 16 Coordinating Conjunctions: 16–4 Appendix, Unit A Basic Grammar Terminology: A–1, A–3, A–4 Appendix, Unit B Questions: B–1	Part I From Grammar to Writing: Avoiding Sentence Fragments Part IX From Grammar to Writing: Avoiding Run-On Sentences and Comma Splices
Chapter 8 Noun Clauses and Using Sources	Chapter 12 Noun Clauses	Unit 10 Noun Clauses: Subjects, Objects, and Complements Unit 11 Direct and Indirect Speech Part IV From Grammar to Writing: Direct and Indirect Speech
Chapter 9 Writing Concisely	Chapter 13 Adjective Clauses Chapter 17 Adverb Clauses: 17–1, 17–2, 17–3, 17–4, 17–5, 17–10 Chapter 18 Reduction of Adverb Clauses to Modifying Adverbial Phrases	Unit 12 Adjective Clauses: Review and Expansion Unit 13 Adjective Clauses with Prepositions; Adjective Phrases Unit 19 Adverb Clauses Unit 20 Adverb and Adverbial Phrases
Chapter 10 Using Academic Vocabulary	–	–

CREDITS

Photos

Pages 2, 32, 70, 73, 84, 108, 128, 138, 153, 155: Shutterstock.com; **Page 15:** Kumar Sriskandan/Alamy; **Page 17:** Woolaroc Museum, Bartlesville, Oklahoma; **Page 26:** iStockphoto.com; **Page 29:** Pictorial Press Ltd/Alamy; **Page 41:** Ivy Close Images/Alamy; **Page 43:** David Hancock/Alamy; **Page 46:** Handout/MCT/Newscom; **Page 60:** UPPA/Photoshot/Newscom; **Page 64:** ZUMA Press/Newscom; **Page 75:** GL Archive/Alamy; **Page 86:** Pictorial Press Ltd/Alamy; **Page 90:** Bettmann/Corbis; **Page 105:** North Wind Picture Archives/Alamy; **Page 123:** David R. Frazier Photolibrary, Inc./Alamy; **Page 126:** Prisma Bildagentur AG/Alamy; **Page 140:** Daily Mail/Rex/Alamy; **Page 141:** Ted Foxx/Alamy; **Page 143:** Peter Frank/Corbis; **Page 152:** Matthew Antonino/Alamy; **Page 157:** Robert Harding Picture Library Ltd/Alamy; **Page 161:** Rob Judges Science/Alamy.

Text

Pages 165–166: "A Moveable Feast" by Laurie McLaughlin. Printed with permission of Titan, The Magazine of California State University at Fullerton; **Pages 167–168:** "Study highlights male bias in animal studies" by Claire Perlman. The Daily Californian, April 20, 2011. Reprinted with Permission; **Pages 169–171:** "Knot just another cap" by Sarah Hall. Copyright © 2011, Firebrand Media LLC. All rights reserved. Reprinted with Permission; **Pages 172–174:** "Zero Tolerance" by Steve Bramucci. Coast Magazine. Reprinted with Permission; **Pages 175–177:** "In economics, cracking the glass ceiling" by Zoe Gorman. Yale Daily News. Printed with Permission; **Pages 178–179:** "Math Made Cool" by Sherry Posnick-Goodwin. Published with permission of the California Educator; **Pages 180–182:** "A Big Heart" by Nicky Vallee. Locale Magazine. Re-birth 2011 pages 31–33. Reprinted with Permission; **Pages 183–185:** "The Rise of Hypochondria" by Lynn Schnurnberger, March/April 2010 © 2010 Lynn Schnurnberger. Initially published in Parade's Healthy Style. All rights reserved. Printed with Permission; **Pages 186–187:** "Making the grade" by Sherry Posnick-Goodwin. Published with permission of the California Educator; **Pages 188–189:** "Students donate the gift of life" by Krysta Fauria. The Hornet, October 20, 2010. Volume 96 Issue 8 Reprinted with Permission.